THE BHS REVISION GUIDE FOR

STAGES 1,2,3 AND THE PTT

Explanatory Note

These revision notes are designed to be read in conjunction with the BHS Training Manuals for Stages 1–3 and the PTT. They do not include notes on the ridden parts of the exams, for which the recommendation is to practise the requirements laid out in the Manuals as much as possible.

The style within these revision notes is to follow the units, learner outcomes and assessment criteria as laid down within the Manuals. Depending upon the requirements and recommendations, the notes may list each assessment criterion individually, or may group them together to give revision notes that are applicable to a range of criteria.

Where assessment criteria for one unit (or for different stages) are identical or very similar to those for another unit, these may be cross-referenced (e.g. 'see **Stage 2, Unit 1a, 1'**).

The
British
Horse
Society

THE BHS REVISION GUIDE FOR

STAGES 1,2,3 AND THE PTT

Jo Winfield FBHS

KENILWORTH PRESS

Copyright © 2014 The British Horse Society

First published in the UK in 2014 by Kenilworth Press, an imprint of Quiller Publishing Ltd

British Library Cataloguing-in-Publication Data
A catalogue record for this book
is available from the British Library

ISBN 978 1 905693 86 3

Line drawings by Dianne Breeze
Cover and book design by Sharyn Troughton
Printed in Malta by Gutenberg Press Ltd.

Kenilworth Press
An imprint of Quiller Publishing
Wykey House, Wykey, Shrewsbury, SY4 1JA
Tel: 01939 261616 Fax: 01939 261606
E-mail: info@quillerbooks.com
Website: www.kenilworthpress.co.uk

Contents

Stage 1 Revision Notes

Unit 1: Brushing off horses including putting on and taking off equipment

1. Be able to work safely and efficiently

1.1–1.4

Exam conditions mean you are working with horses you do not know. Safety is a priority. There is no 'BHS way' of undertaking tasks. As long as it is safe for the horse, yourself and the equipment then the method you use will be up to standard – this is more professionally referred to as 'good practice'.

In this situation you will be looking after a horse who does not belong to you and you may not know. The way you interact with the horses is important. Dealing with a horse like a 'pet' is not professional – instead, deal with the horse firmly but fairly.

Tack and equipment must be safe, and tidiness will help make the yard a safe working place.

Working in a professional and safe way includes being dressed appropriately and completing tasks efficiently, working in a tidy manner, being aware of potential hazards and removing them or avoiding them – i.e. looking after your own health and safety and those of others. You should be aware of, and use, safe and recommended procedures when handling heavy items such as feed sacks, hay bales, etc.

With particular regard to lifting, consider how you lift feed sacks and bales of hay, etc. Remember when lifting a heavy haynet or sack of feed to keep your back straight and bend your knees. If items are especially heavy it is sensible to use wheelbarrows to move feed/bales /haynets across the yard. When lifting and carrying water buckets, carry two at once, one in each hand, to avoid twisting and lifting an uneven load.

It is important to become familiar with these criteria, both from a view of maintaining welfare in practical working situations, and also because they are revisited at times throughout the syllabuses of the Stage exams.

2. Be able to put on a headcollar and tie up the horse correctly and prepare the stable for work

2.1

Take the headcollar, checking it is suitable in size for the horse.

Talk to the horse and let him know you are going to enter.

Open stable door. Go in and close stable door.

2.2

Put on headcollar, ensuring the mane is tidy at the poll and the headcollar is not too high (which may cause rubbing of the protruding cheek bones) or too low (hanging near to nostrils). Make sure the strap of the headcollar is put through the bottom part of the buckle.

2.3

Tie up to string using a quick-release knot. Do not tie too tight (restricting the head movement) or too loose (so there is no control of where the horse moves to). If there is more than one tie ring use one that means the horse's quarters are not immediately behind the door.

2.4–2.5

Skip out the stable before work. Ensure you keep the box skipped out when working around the horse. This will ensure that the bedding stays cleaner and that you and the horse will not tread in the droppings.

If you are going to groom the horse it is worth taking out the water and haynet (if applicable).

3. Be able to brush off/quarter a horse

3.1

Collect the grooming kit and, when not using a brush, ensure the kit stays in the box. The box should be positioned so that you and the horse will not tread on it.

3.2

Pick out the horse's feet into a skip.

Signs the horse needs re-shoeing:

1. Risen clenches.
2. Feet overgrowing the shoe.
3. Shoe worn.

4. Shoe loose.

5. Shoe lost.

3.3

Brushing off is undertaken on a horse who lives out. A dandy brush can be used to get the worst of the mud off, especially where the tack sits on the horse. When using any brush try to use the hand nearer to the horse so you are able to be aware of what his quarters are doing.

Quartering is where a stable-kept horse is brushed to make him tidy for exercise. Undo the rug and fold the front section over his back to expose the front quarter of the horse. Use a body brush to tidy him up and brush out the mane. Bring the rug forward to put it back in position and fold the rear of the rug forwards. Use the body brush again to tidy him up and brush out the tail. If the tail is very fine it may be necessary to use your fingers rather than the body brush. Cover the horse's quarters with the rug and do the rug up.

Your technique must be efficient. Tickling the horse with the brushes will annoy him and will not show efficiency.

4. Know how to groom a horse

4.1

Equipment other than dandy brush and body brush that you may have in the box:

Rubber curry comb – used to remove dirt from a stabled horse.
Plastic curry comb – can be used to remove mud.
Curry comb – used to clean the body brush. Bang on floor to clean out. Never use on a horse.
Wisp/pad – used as part of strapping to bang the horse.
Water brush – for washing off stable stains and to lay the mane.
Stable rubber – used in conjunction with the wisp/pad for banging and for putting on that extra polish.
Three sponges – one for eyes, one for the nose and one for the dock area.
Hoof oil and brush – should not be used daily; only for special occasions.
Tail bandage – used to set the tail after grooming or to protect the tail when travelling.

4.2

Reasons for grooming:
Helps to build up a relationship with the horse.

Removes waste products.
Helps maintain condition.
Promotes health and can help prevent disease.
Helps promote circulation.
Can improve muscle tone.
Improves general appearance.

5. Be able to put on and take off a tail bandage

5.1
Make sure the tail bandage is rolled up correctly, avoid standing against a wall or in a corner; if possible stand slightly to the side of the horse.

The bandage must be put on firmly. Some people find it useful to have a flap at the end of the bandage that can be turned down after a couple of twists.

Try to overlap the bandage the same amount each time you go round the tail. The bandage should go down the tail to the end of the dock (as long as the horse has a normal length dock). The ties should then be tied slightly to the side of the tail – not so near the flesh that it can make the horse sore, but not directly in the middle of the tail as, if travelling, there could be a possibility of the ties rubbing and coming undone. A bow is suitable for tying. The overlap of bandage immediately above the tie can then be pulled down over the bow to aid with security.

5.2
To remove a tail bandage undo the ties and pull the bandage down. If the tail is plaited then you will need to unroll the bandage from the tail.

6. Be able to put on and take off rugs

6.1
You should be able to recognise rugs in everyday use.

Outdoor/turnout rug. These come in a variety of designs, weights and colours. They are designed for horses when they are turned out during colder periods.

Indoor rugs. These come in a greater variety of designs, weights and colours. Modern rugs are lightweight but very effective at keeping horses warm.

Anti-sweat rug. Modern anti-sweat rugs have a wicking effect and draw the sweat away from the horse through the material whilst keeping his body dry.

Day rug. These are not as popular as they used to be. They are smart, woollen rugs that can be used when travelling and at a show.

Summer sheet. This is a thin cotton rug that helps to keep the dust and flies off a horse when travelling or at a show.

6.2

When rugging-up a horse fold the rug in half and gently put it on well forward of the withers. When we are dealing with our own horses we often throw a rug up and over, but we know our horse and his reaction. In an exam you will not know the horse so it is better not to potentially frighten him with the throwing action. Once the rug is on you can then pull it back to the correct position. This ensures the coat is not rubbed up the wrong way.

There are many different ways to attach rugs. Some people say do up the middle straps first; others the breast strap. As long as your horse is tied up, and is sensible and safe, then it does not matter. However, it is better to do up the leg straps last so that you do not go straight to the horse's quarters.

See also item **8.6.**

6.3

To remove the rug:

Talk to the horse.

Check to see if there are leg straps. If there are undo them, but always clip them back to the attachments. Loose straps can catch you in the eye, hit the horse or possibly break a light or window.

Undo the breast strap and then undo the centre straps (nowadays usually cross-over straps).

Fold back the rug and slide off to the side, pulling it over the quarters.

Fold up and put somewhere safe.

7. Be able to put on and take off a saddle, bridle and martingale/hunting breastplate

7.1

If the horse is not tied up then put on his headcollar and tie him up.

Fetch the tack and position it safely. Make sure you have a girth that is likely to fit.

Undo the quick-release knot and leave the rope through the tie string. Undo the headcollar, put it round the horse's neck and do it up.

The tack you are given for Stage 1 should already have been checked for fit for the horse that you are tacking up.

Put the reins and martingale or breastplate over the horse's head and then put the bridle on. The easiest way is to hold both cheekpieces in the right hand over the horse's face. With the left hand guide the bit into the mouth and if necessary put your thumb into the corner of the mouth to encourage the horse to open it. Lift the right hand to lift the bit into the horse's mouth and put the headpiece carefully over the ears. Ensure the mane is tidy under the headpiece and pull the forelock from under the browband. You could now remove the headcollar if you want to, but do not drop it on the floor. Loop it through the tie ring so neither you nor the horse can get caught up in it. Twist the reins and put one of them up through the throatlash, making sure the throatlash is not too tight.

Do up the noseband and make sure it is level on the horse's face. If it is a cavesson noseband it is usually done up so you can get at least one finger comfortably between it and the horse's face. A flash noseband needs to be at the same height as a cavesson noseband but needs to be tight enough so that the flash strap does not pull it down over the nose. If you have not already put the headcollar back on then do so now.

If the horse has a rug on and it is cold just fold the rug back and leave it on to help to keep his loins warm.

7.2–7.4

Make sure the girth is either slipped through the offside stirrup iron or is safely placed over the skirt of the saddle. Put the numnah on well forward and pull it up at the withers. Put the saddle on to the numnah and slide both of them into the correct position. (If you push down on the pommel of the saddle it should slide into the correct position.) Check that the saddle does not look too far forward over the withers or too far back onto the loins. Also make sure you can see the numnah all the way round the saddle. It is sensible to lift the numnah up into the pommel of the saddle. Go to the offside of the horse and check the numnah on that side. Put the girth down and lift the saddle flap to ensure the girth is done up and the buckle guards are covering the buckles of the girth. Come back to the nearside, put the martingale or breastplate strap through the girth and do it up. Historically the girth is done up on the first and third straps (because of the way in which the straps were attached to the saddle) but which straps you use can vary. Just have a good reason for choosing the ones you do. Ensure that the girth is tight enough so that the saddle does not slip. Make sure the martingale loop is central between the horse's forelegs.

If there is a breastplate to work with then attach the loops on either side of the horse's withers to the attachment points on the saddle. If there is a choice of attachments use the one that is attached directly to the tree of the saddle as this is less likely to break than one that is attached by a small piece of leather.

If you have to wait for the assessor and it is cold, bring the rug back up over the saddle.

7.5

To untack it is easier to take the saddle off first as you have the martingale/breastplate to deal with. You may need to take the rug off before doing this.

Undo the girth and slide out the martingale loop. Do not drop the girth as it might hit the horse's legs. Undo the breastplate straps on both sides (if applicable), slide the saddle back and lift it onto your right arm and collect the girth with your left. Put the saddle somewhere safe. Undo the headcollar and place it safely (if you are not sure you can control the horse you can put it round his neck again), undo the noseband and the throatlash. Stand facing forwards and lift the headpiece over the horse's ears and gently let the bit slide out of his mouth. Hold the bridle over your arm and then put the headcollar on. Then bring the reins and martingale over the horse's head. If you feel you can control the horse in the stable then you could take the bridle off completely before you put the headcollar on, but you should never do this when you are not in an enclosed area.

Make sure the tack is safe and put the horse's rug back on if he was wearing one. He can then be let loose in the box.

8. Know about tack and rugs

8.1

Know the names of the parts of the saddle and bridle.

8.2

Tack should:

Appear soft and supple.

Be clean.

Not be cracked.

Not be worn where metal and leather touch.

Have adjustment holes that are not stretched or split.

8.3

Worn or dirty tack:

Can rub the horse and cause galls/sores.

Can break and cause an accident.

Is unsightly and gives the appearance of the rider not caring.

8.4

Securing a noseband: the correct fitting of a noseband is described under **7.1** – putting on a bridle with a noseband.

8.5

To clean tack you need:

Warm water.

Cloths and sponges.

Saddle soap (there are many different types of soaps).

Hook to hang tack on.

Ideally use a saddle horse for the saddle.

For a special clean – metal polish and duster.

Process:

Take the tack apart and check for wear and tear.

Wash the bit and stirrup irons.

Wash tack with small amount of warm water to remove grease and dirt.

Rub saddle soap into all leather areas and both sides. If the soap is in the form of a bar do not get it too wet so that it creates a lather.

For a special occasion clean the buckles and stirrups with metal polish and polish with a duster.

Put the tack back together and hang up.

8.6

When fitting a rug, the rug should cover the horse's quarters and be deep enough to keep his body warm. Round the shoulders it should fit snugly, but not so tight that it pinches. Make sure the straps are all taut enough to keep the rug in place. If, at this point in the exam, you notice that the rug is not a perfect fit, carry on and fit the rug but be prepared to discuss your concerns with the assessor when they come and talk to you.

Unit 2: Horse husbandry, identification and handling

1. Be able to work safely and efficiently

1.1–1.4
Throughout all the assessments you are expected to undertake tasks in a manner that is safe for you, the horse and the equipment you are using, i.e. developing best practice. This will not only be helpful for passing your exams, but will ensure you become safe, efficient and employable and will be appreciated wherever you work. Tidiness will help make the yard a safe working place.
For further details on the key criteria, refer to **Stage 1, Unit 1,1–4.**

2. Be able to skip out and set fair a bed

2.1–2.2
Always skip out the horse once he is tied up and keep him skipped out as you are working with him. Depending on the type of bedding there are various ways you can skip out. If you take a long-handled fork into the box make sure you do not prod the horse – the best way to do this is by making sure one hand is always over the end of the fork. This also helps your back. If you use a skip/poop-a -scoop make sure you move the horse over so you are safe. Try to take out all of the droppings whilst removing the smallest amount of bed.
'Set fair' may seem an old-fashioned term. It just means to tidy the bed up. Again what you do depends on the type of bedding. If there are straw or shavings banks you need to ensure the banks are high and thick enough. The area in front of the stable door needs to be tidied so there is less likelihood of bedding being dragged out onto the yard. The droppings need skipping out and the water refreshing. If more bedding needs to be added, then you should comment on this, but there may not be time in the exam to actually do this. Remember if there is a horse in the box he must be tied up. It is always safer, if possible, to remove the horse when mucking out and setting fair.

3. Know about bedding and how to utilise it for the horse's comfort and safety

3.1 – 3.2
Types of bedding:
Straw is warm and comfortable and provides good drainage. It is absorbent. On the muck

heap it rots well and is easily disposed of. It is not good for horses with respiratory problems. To look after a straw bed all of the soiled bedding should be removed and the banks turned regularly to avoid it becoming musty. If a deep litter bed is used then just the droppings should be removed daily; the stable will then have a full muck-out at the end of the season. Deep litter is good for barning and yarding horses rather than stabling.

Wheat straw – used to be cheap, but not so any more.

Barley straw – can have 'awns' on the end that may make it prickly.

Oat straw – tends to be eaten.

Shavings can be expensive and sometimes not available. Good for horses with respiratory problems as long as of good quality and dust free. It takes a long time to rot down and difficult to dispose of. To look after a shavings bed the droppings and soiled area should be mucked out in the morning and the droppings skipped out throughout the day; this allows the bedding to be used efficiently with minimal wastage. A specific shavings fork is required to work the bedding.

Paper is dust free, but can make the yard untidy, can be difficult to work with when wet and is difficult to dispose of. Newsprint can leave marks on grey horses. Some centres have a machine that produces their own paper bedding from newspapers brought in by clients.

Hemp is produced from the hemp plant. It is very absorbent and dust free, but very expensive. Rots down very well and can be sold to gardeners. A shavings fork can be used and the bedding should be managed in a similar manner to shavings.

Peat should not be used nowadays because sourcing it is considered to be damaging to the environment. if it is used, the droppings and soiled areas need to be removed as per other bedding types.

Wood fibre is environmentally friendly, being made from recycled white wood fibre. It is fairly dust free, free-draining and can leave top surface dry. Warm and comfortable. Manage as per shavings.

Wood pellets are a wood fibre product that has been heat-treated and compressed. Installed by putting the bed down and adding water. (The amount of water will vary, so it is often easier to spread out the pellets in the stable and then spray with a hosepipe and allow to absorb; more water can then be applied as required.) The pellets expand and are very absorbent. Dust free and rot down quickly.

Rubber matting is initially expensive to install. Rubber matting should never be used without a small amount of bedding to soak up waste. Horses left on rubber matting without any bedding may not wish to stale. It is better for the matting not to be sealed to the ground so it can be lifted up and the floor cleaned and disinfected regularly. It saves on bedding costs and mucking out is done quickly. Assuming that a covering of shavings is used, manage as per shavings.

3.3

Mucking out is best done when the horse is not in the stable.

If horse has to stay in its box, then tie him up.

Leave the tools outside the stable until you need them.

If you are using long-handled tools then learn to keep one hand over the end of the handle. This will ensure you do not prod the horse with the handle, and will help to keep your back safe.

Skip out the visible droppings using a suitable skip (depending on the type of bedding).

Sort bedding and throw clean bedding to one side.

Remove wet bedding.

Sweep the floor.

Put the bed back down.

Some yards put clean straw to top up the bed straight after mucking out. Others wait until the afternoon to top up.

If the bed has banks, one bank per day should be turned and tidied.

Deep litter system:

The bed is skipped out in the morning and throughout the day. It has a complete muck out regularly. This is a labour-saving way to keep a bed (until you have to take everything out). The bed tends to be warm and it uses less bedding. However, it is less hygienic than mucking out daily and the horses' feet must be watched very carefully for thrush.

3.4

There are several different ways that manure can be stored prior to being taken away. The traditional method is to build a muck heap in three sections on a concrete base. There may be walls at the sides and to separate the heap into three parts. One section is the freshest muck that is being added to daily, the second is a section that is being rotted down and the third is a well-rotted section that is ready to be taken away. All three piles should be neatly stacked, square and flat. They should be well trodden down to assist the anaerobic bacteria (bacteria that work without air) to break down the manure.

Many yards have a contractor who leaves a large trailer into which the manure can be wheeled daily. Once the trailer is full they will collect it and leave another empty one.

No matter how the muck is stored and collected, the area and the heap should be kept tidy.

If you have another method of storing manure at your yard then talk about that way in your exam.

The muck heap should be downwind from the yard and far enough away so that flies will not bother the horses, but convenient enough to allow for frequent trips as required.

4. Be able to correctly identify the points, colours and markings of a horse

4.1

The points of a horse.

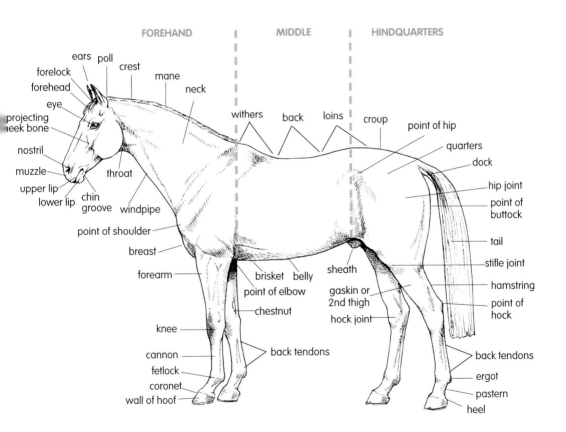

4.2 – 4.3

Colours:

Bay – light or dark brown with black points (points are the mane, tail and bottom of the legs).

Brown – any shade of brown all over the body (except for white markings).

Black – black all over body.

Chestnut – reddish or ginger all over the body (except for white markings).

Liver chestnut – darker than chestnut.

Dun – gold or 'mouse' colour with black points. Often has a black dorsal stripe (black line of hair following the line of the vertebrae).

Palomino – gold or cream in colour with a similar coloured mane and tail.

Grey – white or white and black hairs mixed.

Types of grey – in a *dappled grey* the dapples are small circles of black/black and white hairs sometimes on the neck and quarters only, sometimes over the whole body. As the horse grows older the coat usually loses its dapples and becomes either a *'flea-bitten'* grey where dark hairs appear in tufts, or loses the darker hair altogether. An *iron grey* is a dark grey horse. Again as the horse becomes older the colour will become lighter.

Appaloosa – an appaloosa is a spotted horse. There are different types of appaloosa depending on where the spots occur and the size of them.

Piebald – a horse with black and white patches.

Skewbald – any horse of any colour but black, with white patches.

Roan – A roan is a horse who has hairs of mixed colour. *Strawberry roan*– chestnut and white hairs mixed. *Blue roan* – black and white hairs mixed. *Bay roan* – brown and white hairs mixed.

Albino – pink skin covered with white hair. An albino has pink eyes. A true albino is quite rare.

5. Be able to hold and lead a horse for treatment or inspection

5.1

When holding a horse for treatment you should stand on the same side as the vet. If the horse moves away from the vet he will not knock into you.

When holding a horse for somebody to inspect, stand to the front and just to the side of the horse so you don't block their view, but you will not get knocked over if he shoots forward.

5.2

When leading a horse stand by his shoulder on the nearside and try to push him past you with a straight arm. Do not try to pull a horse. If you need to encourage the horse forward use your whip in your left hand behind you and try to touch him behind the girth area. Do not look at the horse, as this is likely to back him off. Be positive and think forward yourself. When trotting, apply the same method and try to run in time with the horse's legs.

5.3

When turning a horse you are leading, always turn him away from you (to the right). This stops him stepping on you and allows the observer to watch the horse's legs without you getting in the way.

6. Know how to use a haynet

6.1

Open the net and drape it on the floor. Shake the hay into the net or place the slices from a bale into it. Weigh it with a spring balance.

6.2

If the net is tied too low the horse may get a foot caught in it when empty. Haynets have also occasionally been known to get stuck between horses' teeth. If the horse is prone to getting caught in the haynet then tie a piece of baling twine to the wall attachment and secure the haynet to this. On tension this will break. Otherwise, feed the hay on the floor or from a manger.

7. Be able to tie up a haynet

7.1

Make sure the quick-release knot is turned towards the wall. Not everybody likes to use a haynet as the horse's head and neck are not in a natural position for eating.

Unit 3: The principles of caring for horses

1. Know the basic principles of health, safety and welfare when working with horses

1.1

Suitable clothes when working with horses.

Yard work:

Warm, waterproof jacket and trousers if working outside in inclement weather.

Strong waterproof footwear.

Hard hat and gloves available if you need to move or handle horses.

A hat or scarf will help to keep you warm.

Long hair is better tied back.

Personal Protective Equipment (PPE) when required – e.g. mask for working with hay.

No jewellery.

Riding:

Jodhpurs or breeches.

Hat to recognised kite mark standard.

Gloves.

Riding boots.

It is better to keep your arms covered, especially when riding outside.

No jewellery.

1.2

It is important to be fit enough to undertake yard work. If not, you are liable to injure yourself especially when you get tired. Working with horses involves long hours of physical work in all weathers. If you are not prepared to do this then perhaps you should reconsider your decision to work with horses.

1.3

It is the responsibility of everybody on the yard to ensure their personal safety. Understanding fire precautions is part of this.

Fire precautions:

No smoking anywhere on the yard.

Keep passageways clear.

Do not leave tools lying around.

Each horse should have his own headcollar outside his box.

Everyone should know how to use the fire extinguishers, and where they are.

Everyone should know the fire procedure for your yard – this usually involves:

- Alerting everybody to the fire.
- Dialling 999 and asking for the Fire Brigade.
- Gathering at the fire point and checking everybody is accounted for.
- Getting the horses out and put into the designated field – first move the horses nearest to the fire (if safe to do so).

The proprietor/chief instructor will tell you what to do next.

1.4

Basic accident procedure:

Keep calm. Assess the situation. Make sure it is safe for you to approach. Make the areas safe to prevent any further accidents. Check for any additional hazards such as a loose horse, unsafe equipment – cables, furniture or elements – water, fire, etc.

Assess the casualty; follow first aid procedure and guidance.

Send for help; call 999 if an ambulance/police/fire brigade are required.

Fill out necessary accident report forms and paperwork as soon as possible.

1.5

When leading a horse on the road:

Make sure the horse has a bridle on.

Walk on the left-hand side of the road.

Be observant.

Place yourself between the horse and the traffic (on the horse's offside).

Make sure you and the horse are wearing reflective clothing.

When riding on the road:

Make sure the horse's tack and shoes are safe.

You and the horse should wear reflective clothing.

Be observant.

Never ride more than two abreast; on narrow roads ride in single file.

Ride on the left-hand side of the road.

If taking a horse ride and lead have the lead horse nearest to the kerb.

Thank traffic that slows down.

It is sensible not to ride out on the road at busy rush hour times or when the weather and visibility are poor, such as in snow and ice and foggy conditions.

1.6
Role of the BHS:
Lead charity for the promotion of welfare of the horse through education.
Prevention of cruelty and neglect to horses through welfare support and advice.
Provides training and examinations in riding and stable management.
Promotes the ridden and driven rights of way and access of the public roads, highways, footpaths, bridleways
Third Party insurance for horse owners.

2. Know the signs of good and ill health in a horse and understand basic behaviour and welfare

2.1
What to look for at morning and evening inspections.
Morning:
If the horse usually welcomes you over the door, but doesn't this morning, this requires investigation.
Check the horse for injury.
Ensure that food has been eaten and normal amount of water drunk.
Check the bed is no more disturbed than usual.
Check number of droppings is normal.
Make sure rugs are tidy.

Evening:
Make sure horse's behaviour is normal.
Top up water.
Top up the haynet and re-secure.
Skip out.
Check rugs are fitted comfortably.
Make sure stable door is secure.
Set alarm (if applicable).
Switch off lights.

2.2
Signs of good health:
Temperature normal (100–101 °F) (38 °C).
Pulse normal (36–42 beats per minute).
Respiration normal (8–15 breaths per minute).

Good condition.

Alert and interested in what is going on.

Shiny coat.

Bright eyes.

Droppings break on touching the ground and are of normal amount.

Signs of ill health:

Rise or fall in temperature, pulse and respiration (not related to work or exercise).

Poor condition.

Dull coat.

Loose or hard droppings or lack of droppings.

Discharge from nose.

Sweating.

Coughing.

Not wanting to eat or drink.

Looking uncomfortable.

Heat/swelling.

Lameness.

Obvious injury.

Rolling excessively.

2.3

If anything appears not to be normal then report it immediately to a senior member of staff. After evening stables the horse is left alone until the morning and something that appears small and trivial can be a major issue by the time morning stables are undertaken.

2.4

The horse's lifestyle in the wild can be summarised as follows.

The horse has three basic instincts in this order:

– To survive.

– To nourish.

– To reproduce.

He is a creature of flight and would rather run away than fight. If he is cornered he will fight by using his hind legs, his teeth and his forelegs when rearing.

He is a herd animal – there is safety in numbers.

The herd will roam in search of food. They eat little and often. This is called trickle feeding. They try to find water two or three times a day. Their feet are worn down by crossing over a variety of terrain and their manes and tails are long to help keep them warm. The natural grease in their coats also helps to keep them warm. Loose hair is removed by rolling and mutual grooming.

2.5

A horse's body language can tell you a lot about how he feels. This can be very helpful in identifying dangerous behavioural signs.

 If his ears are flat back then he is likely to be very angry and may well be ready to attack, be it with teeth or hooves. If he is 'twitchy' and/or his tail is clamped down he may be nervous and so feel the need to protect himself. If his eyes are big and staring he may well have seen something that has frightened him.

If he is frightened when he is in a field he may well run away from what has caused his fear and, when he feels he is far enough away, he will turn round, look and possibly snort.

If he is frightened in a stable he may go into the corner. His head will then be protected and he can use his hind legs to kick out.

If he is frightened when being ridden he may well try to bolt from whatever has caused the fear.

3. Know how to maintain a horse in a safe grazing environment

3.1

Daily checks in a field:
Water.
Fencing.
Gate/security.
Amount of grass.
Poisonous plants.
Horses for injuries.
Rabbit holes.
Pick up droppings.

3.2

Turning out, handling and catching.

Turning out a horse:
If the horse is sensible, put on his headcollar. If he gets excited, or has not been turned out for some time, then use a bridle. Wear riding hat and gloves. Lead the horse to the

field. Take him through the gate into the field and shut the gate behind you. Turn the horse so his head is facing the gate. Take off the headcollar/bridle. Do not turn your back on the horse. Watch him move away.

If leading more than one horse at a time then the same process should be utilised. Communicate with the other people turning out and make sure you all take the headcollars off at the same time.

Catching a horse:

If catching one horse in a group do not take a bucket of food – you will be overwhelmed by horses. Wear riding hat and gloves. Take a titbit in your pocket. Carry the headcollar behind your back and walk up to the horse, approaching his shoulder. Put the rope round his neck and then put the headcollar on. Once you are away from the other horses you can reward him.

3.3

A horse-sick field is identified by:

- Being overgrazed
- Areas of lawns (grazed right down) and long, rank grass (where there are droppings)
- Droppings not picked up or harrowed. Harrowing tends to be carried out in larger pastures where droppings are not easily picked up. It is best to do this in dry, sunny conditions; doing so in damp, humid conditions may simply spread worm larvae.

If a field is in such condition (showing little management) then it may also have:

- Poor-quality fencing
- Gates that do not work freely
- Poisonous plants
- Rabbit holes
- A water supply that is inadequate (e.g. buckets or an old bath that needs to be filled daily)

3.4

The main reason for a field becoming horse-sick is over grazing. To cure this, the field needs to be rested. The long, rank grass needs cutting or grazing with sheep or cattle, and the droppings spread. (There will probably be too many to pick up.)

Once the field has recovered make sure the droppings are picked up daily. If the field is big enough it could be split so that each half could be rested for three weeks at a time to allow the grass to grow. Picking up the droppings will also help to keep the worm burden to a minimum.

4. Know how to feed and water horses

4.1

Rules of feeding and watering:

- Feed according to the work being undertaken, body weight, age, temperament, weather conditions.
- Feed little and often (this mimics how the horse would feed in the wild because of his small stomach).
- Do not change feed type suddenly (there will not be enough specific bacteria in the gut to break down a large amount of the new food type as each food type has its own bacteria).
- Feed plenty of fibre.
- Keep all feeding utensils and bins very clean.
- Keep to a regular feeding routine.
- Use only good-quality feed (horses may not eat poor-quality food, and if they do it could cause colic or respiratory disorders).
- Feed something succulent daily.
- Do not give a full feed to an exhausted horse.
- Do not work for at least an hour after a full feed.
- A constant supply of fresh, clean water should always be available.
- If a horse has not had water for some time then offer small amounts frequently: in such circumstances do not allow him to drink as much as he wants.
- Water before feeding – this rule is somewhat outdated now as horses have free access to water and so tend not to drink a lot after feeding. It comes from the days when horses were taken to a trough to drink.

4.2

Identifying common types of feed and forage:
You should be able to identify a range of feed types.

Assessing quality of feed:
To assess the quality of a feed sample check it is not faded in colour, dusty or musty. Many (but not all) feed samples in jars have been there for some considerable time and would not be suitable for feeding to a horse.

4.3

Feed cleanliness:
It is very important that the feed room is kept clean and tidy so as not to attract vermin.

Feed should be kept in metal or heavy-duty plastic bins so that vermin cannot come into contact with it.

Mangers/feed bowls must be kept clean – horses may be put off by stale food in their feed containers. This could lead to a lack of condition and is wasting money. Eating old/contaminated feed can cause colic. Would you like to eat your food from a dirty plate?

Feed quality:
Feeding poor-quality feed of any type potentially leads to digestive issues like colic. It is a waste of money. Although it may be cheaper than good-quality forage the horse will not benefit as much, or might not eat it at all. Feeding dusty or mouldy hay/haylage can lead to respiratory disorders (and, in the case of haylage, may be potentially toxic) and again can be waste of money.

4.4
When establishing any daily feeding regime it is important to remember that each horse is an individual and the basic rules are only a starting point. Keep a close eye on the horse's behaviour, condition and weight and adjust the feeding regime accordingly. That said, the following general points will prove helpful.

Grass-kept horse in light work:
Spring: grazing may need to be restricted if there is plenty of grass in order to keep laminitis and obesity at bay. If the horse is to stand in a box for any length of time then some hay or haylage will be required.

Summer: the grass may well be sufficient to work the horse from. If there is not much grass and he is working regularly, then he may need a small hard feed when brought in. Horse and pony nuts or a coarse mix would be best to use as these provide a complete balanced diet.

Autumn: during early autumn there can be another flush of grass, so a close watch must be kept and, if necessary grazing, may need to be restricted again. As the goodness of the grass starts to diminish later in the autumn it may be necessary to start to supplement the grass with hay/haylage. Remember to always put out at least one more pile than the number of horses in the field so that the one at the bottom of the pecking order has always got feed to go to.

Winter: it may be necessary to feed hay twice a day and give a small hard feed daily. If it is icy, any ice on water troughs needs to be broken twice a day. Feeding hard feed to a group of horses in a field can be difficult and is potentially dangerous. It is better if the horses can be brought into stables for this. If not, it may be worth considering bringing the horses out of the field and them being held, one person per horse, whilst they are eating from feed bowls.

Stabled horse in light work:
It is always better to turn out a horse for as long a time as possible. The amount of forage and hard feed can be adjusted according to the amount of grass and its quality that the horse has access to.
A horse should be fed 2½ per cent of his bodyweight per day. The only way to measure this scientifically is to use a weighbridge. Without a weighbridge a rough guide for the total amount that should be fed per day is:

16hh – 30lb (13.6.kg)
15hh – 26lb (11.8.kg)
14hh – 22lb (10.0kg)
13hh – 18lb (8.2kg)
12hh – 14lb (6.4kg)

From these figures a 16hh horse undertaking light work should receive about 30lb (13.6kg) per day. Most horses would undertake light work quite happily on 10 per cent hard feed and 90 per cent bulk feed. That is about 3lb (1.36kg) of hard feed and 27lb (12.24kg) of bulk. Some horses may need up to 15 per cent hard feed for light work, but rarely any more than that. For the hard feed it is better to use nuts or coarse mix as you are giving the horse a complete balanced diet.
Always remember every horse is an individual.

4.5
Methods of feeding and watering.
In a field:
When feeding hay, always put out more piles of hay than there are horses, so that there is always a pile for a bullied horse to go to. They should be far enough apart so horses cannot kick each other. Hard feed is better not fed in the field with a group of horses.
When providing water, note that:
- Large troughs that refill automatically are best; troughs that are not automatic need to be refilled daily.
- Old baths can be dangerous if sharp edges are not boxed in.
- Buckets can be knocked over.
- Provision is best kept away from gateways and overhanging trees.

In the stable:

It is natural for the horse to put his head down to eat, so hard feed is best fed in a feed bowl on the ground. The feed bowl can then be removed and cleaned thoroughly before the next feed.

Permanent breast-high mangers are difficult to keep clean.

As with hard feed, hay may also be best fed on the ground. However, if the horse tends to waste the hay then a haynet may be necessary. This must be tied high enough so that the horse cannot get his foot caught in it when the net is empty.

When providing water, note that:

- Buckets are easily cleaned and refilled, but also easily knocked over/broken. They provide a means by which it is easy to add medication to the water if required to do so by vet, and offer a ready way of identifying how much a horse has drunk.
- Automatic waterers are potentially labour-saving and should provide a constant supply of water. However, they are not always cleaned frequently enough and can freeze in winter unless well insulated. It is not easy to add medicine to water supplied by this means and you cannot tell how much a horse is drinking (unless individual monitors are added, which is expensive).

Stage 2 Revision Notes

Unit 1a: Groom and plait horses and fit equipment

1. Be able to work safely and efficiently

1.1–1.3

As in all units it is important to work safely. The way in which you handle the horses and equipment will always be taken into consideration. You must not put yourself into a potentially dangerous situation. Make sure you keep equipment tidy and safe. For all units you will be expected to work in a timely fashion that is acceptable to industry.

2. Know procedures for working safely on a yard

2.1

Keep calm. Assess the situation. Make sure it is safe for you to approach. Make the areas safe to prevent any further accidents. This may involve catching a loose horse or removing anything that may be a potential hazard, such as a ladder / bales etc – but only if they are safe to move.

Seek immediate help and assistance; if on your own then assess the casualty; follow first aid procedure and guidance.

Send for help; call 999 if an ambulance/police required.

Fill out necessary accident report forms and paperwork as soon as possible.

2.2

Some ways of working safely on a yard:

Obey the yard rules.

Be observant.

Use tools correctly.

Do not leave tools around.

Be tidy in your work.

Work as a team with other staff.

Listen carefully to instructions.

Always tie up a horse when working with him.
Do not take a wheelbarrow into a box if a horse is inside.

3. Be able to strap a horse

3.1–3.2

Strapping is a thorough grooming of a horse which is usually undertaken after exercise when the pores of the skin are open. Part of strapping is banging the horse.
Collect grooming kit.
Put on headcollar and tie up horse.
Pick out feet into a skip.
Use body brush and curry comb over the body.
When brushing the head undo the quick-release knot and put the headcollar round the neck. Brush the forelock out at the same time.
Brush the mane by putting it to the side other than the one it falls on, brush along the crest and the underside of the mane, and then bring it back over in small sections so each part is thoroughly groomed.
If the tail is fine it may be better to use the fingers gently so that the hairs are not broken.
Always stand in a safe position to the side of the horse and do not be cornered.
Then take a wisp/massage pad and a stable rubber and bang the horse. Put the wisp into the brushing hand and the stable rubber in the other. Only bang on the parts of the body where the muscles are; do not bang the bony areas.

Banging (some people use the actual term strapping although this is the complete groom) needs to be introduced gently. Do not go up to a horse you do not know and use the pad strongly. Come down onto the muscle with the pad, lift it off and then wipe the area with the stable rubber. As the horse gets used to it you can become stronger with your 'slap' of the pad. After five or six slaps and wipes in a rhythm lift the pad as if to make contact, but do not. The muscles should contract (in preparation for the contact). This is the main function of banging – to make the muscle work and so build up the amount a horse has. It is also good to promote circulation, help with relaxation and cleanliness.
If it is cold the horse's rug can be left on his quarters until you are ready to bang them.

4. Know the process of grooming a rugged-up horse

4.1

Prior to exercise:
The horse should be groomed to remove the stable stains and bedding from the coat;

31

this is an important time to check for any lumps/bumps and injury that may have occurred overnight. Always groom without any gloves on so that you can assess by feel the state of the horse's legs and coat.

Collect grooming kit and proceed as for 3.1 and 3.2. The horse should have his body groomed with the body brush and curry comb to quickly brush over the whole body, taking care over bony or ticklish regions such as the head and under the stomach and between the hind legs.

Remove any stable stains with a sponge and water.

The horse should have his feet picked out, mane and tail brushed through before tacking up for exercise.

After exercise:

The horse should have any excessive sweat, mud and dirt washed off by hose or bucket and sponge. This is best done while the horse is still warm from having been ridden. He should then have a suitable rug on whilst being allowed to dry off.

To groom thoroughly after exercise the horse should be completely dry and cool. The process would follow as per strapping and banging.

In addition the tail may be bandaged (with the bandage being removed after a few hours), hooves oiled, and stable rugs applied for the evening.

5. Be able to plait the mane and tail with elastic bands/thread

5.1–5.3

Collect the equipment and tie up the horse. If using a needle it may be better to see if the horse can be tied outside.

Plaiting a mane:

Brush the mane and split into the number of plaits required using elastic bands to ensure each plait will be the same size. It is traditional to have an odd number of plaits down the neck with the forelock making an even number in total.

Damp down the section to be plaited.

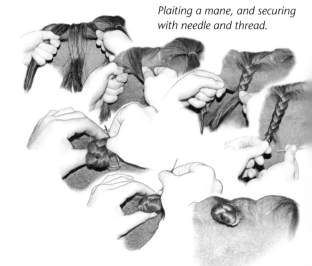

Plaiting a mane, and securing with needle and thread.

Some people say it is better to start at the poll. If the horse gets impatient later on, it is easier to plait lower down the neck.

Plaiting a tail:
Make sure the horse is tied up and you have plenty of room.
Brush out the tail and then damp the dock area down.

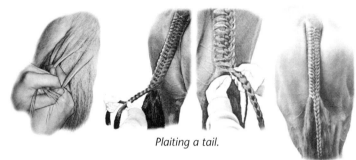

Plaiting a tail.

6. Be able to prepare a horse for travelling

6.1

Select and fit suitable rugs and equipment for the size of horse, the weather and the type of journey that may be undertaken.

When fitting travel boots make sure that you have them the right way up and that the Velcro does up from the inside towards the outside of the horse. Some makes like Woof boots have a 'W' on them and you can tell if they are the right way up by making sure the letter is a 'W' and not an 'M' before putting them on.

Travel equipment should fit the horse. Equipment that is too big is potentially dangerous as it may start to come off and may panic the horse. Equipment that is too small will not be functional or again may come undone.

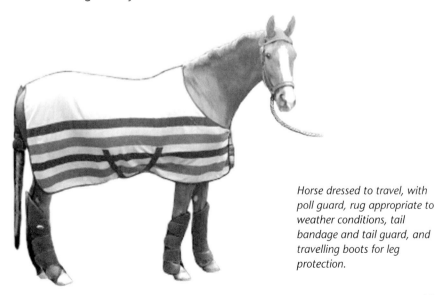

Horse dressed to travel, with poll guard, rug appropriate to weather conditions, tail bandage and tail guard, and travelling boots for leg protection.

33

6.2

Bandaging.

Stable bandage – padding
just below the bandage, to
prevent unnecessary
interference with bedding

Travel bandage – more
padding for protection, and
padding lower to protect
coronary band

7. Know procedures for fitting and storing clothing and equipment

7.1
When fitting clothing and equipment the size of the horse and the use of the clothing and equipment should be taken into consideration.

7.2–7.4
With rugs made of synthetic materials it is relatively easy to put them in the washing machine to clean them. It is best to wash off any stable stains first. If you only have a small washing machine then there are numerous companies that will wash and reproof your rugs for you.

It is best to get any repairs done before the rugs are put away so that they will be ready to use when they are required. They should be stored in a dry place, secure so that moths and vermin cannot get at them.

Tack not being used should be cleaned and then stored safely in a dry environment.

To ensure you get the maximum use from your equipment you should clean it regularly and check for repairs that need to be done. If repairs are undertaken early then the equipment will last longer and be safer for horse and rider. Keeping equipment safe and clean will expand its lifespan and save you money.

Unit 1b: Fit, remove and maintain tack for exercise

1. Be able to fit and remove tack needed for exercise

1.1
You will be asked to tack up a horse for exercise and to fit the tack.
Go into the stable with a headcollar. Fit the headcollar and tie up the horse with a quick-release knot.
Skip out the box. You may also wish to take out the haynet.

1.2
Check the approximate size of the horse and then select what you think will be appropriate tack.
You will be asked also to fit a running martingale or breastplate and boots.

Bridle:
Take the leather out of the keepers.
Hold the bridle up to the horse's head to check it is an approximate fit.
Undo the lead rope and leave through the string.
Put the headcollar round the horse's neck.
Put on the bridle.
Quickly adjust the cheek pieces if necessary. Generally it is accepted that the height of the bit should just make the horse's lips 'smile'.
Make sure the mane at the poll is comfortable and the forelock is pulled out from under the browband.
Make sure the browband and noseband are straight and that the browband is not too close to the ears.
Put straps back into keepers.
Do up the noseband.

Put on the breastplate or martingale:
Check for fit across the withers, under the chest and the length of running straps (if a running martingale).
Twist the reins several times and put one rein up through the throatlash and do it up.
Put the headcollar on over the bridle and redo the quick-release knot.

Saddle:
Try the saddle on the horse's back to see if it fits.

Remove the saddle and put on the numnah, well forward.

Put the saddle on the numnah – pull the numnah into the arch at the pommel of the saddle and slide them both back with the heel of your palm until the saddle is in the right place.

Attached the numnah straps to the saddle.

Go to the offside and check you can see the numnah all the way round the saddle and then put the girth through the numnah loop.

Go to the nearside and also check you can see the numnah all the way round the saddle. Reach for the girth and put the breastplate/martingale strap through it.

Do up the girth, ensuring it is through the numnah loop. The girth should be tight enough so that the saddle is safe.

Attach the breastplate (if fitted) to the saddle. If there are two sets of rings use the ones that are attached directly to the tree of the saddle. If there is a martingale then untwist the reins and put the rings through the reins making sure they 'run'.

At rest, the martingale should not exert any downward pressure on the reins; it should come into action only when the horse puts his head above the angle of control.

A correctly fitted running martingale.

Noseband:

Check for the fit of the noseband according to its type. If it is a cavesson noseband it is generally accepted that you should be able to get two fingers between it and the horse's skin. If it is a flash noseband the flash strap should not be tighter than the cavesson part of the noseband. This will pull the cavesson down.

1.3

Fit brushing boots all round. If they have single straps, make sure that they go from front to back and are tight enough so they will not come off when the horse is working. There are many different types of brushing boot nowadays and it is important to look at the shape of the boot at the fetlock to ensure they are put on correctly. Always make sure the fetlocks are protected and the boots are not put on too high.

1.4

The procedure for untacking is as follows.

Take off the boots. Undo them from bottom to top. This makes it easier and they are less likely to fall on the floor.

If you have a martingale/breastplate it is more efficient to take the saddle off first. Undo the breastplate attachments on both sides. Undo the girth and slip out the breastplate/martingale loop.

Slide the saddle and numnah along the horse's back a little way and lift it off onto your right arm.

With your left hand, reach for the girth and bring it over onto the seat of the saddle.

Put the saddle somewhere safe. As the horse is tied up you can put it on the stable door. If you need to put it on the ground make sure you put it down on its pommel and bring the girth up over the cantle to protect the leather from whatever you are leaning it against.

Undo the lead rope and leave the end through the loop.

Take off the headcollar. Do not drop it on the floor.

Undo the noseband and throatlash.

Stand by the side of the horse and face forward.

Put one arm under the horse's throat and with both hands lift the headpiece carefully over the ears.

Gently let the bridle down so the horse can let go of the bit and not knock his teeth. To pull a bridle off forward can lead to the horse's teeth being knocked by the bit.

Put the headcollar back on.

Bring the reins and martingale/breastplate over the horse's ears.

You will need to unclip the lead rope to bring the reins through. Clip the rope back up. If the horse had a rug on then replace it.

2. Be able to work safely

2.1

Throughout all the assessments you are expected to undertake tasks in a manner that is safe for you, the horse and the equipment you are using. In other words, developing best practice. This will not only be helpful for passing your exams, but will ensure you become safe, efficient and employable and will be appreciated wherever you work.

For further details see **Stage 1, Unit 1, 1.1–1.4.**

3. Be able to select, use and maintain tack

3.1

Check the approximate size of the horse and then select what you think will be appropriate tack. Check the stitching, and any signs of wear and tear that would make the tack unsuitable for the safety of horse/rider, the fit and the comfort of the horse.

3.2

Tack should be cleaned regularly.

The bit should be washed off immediately after use to remove saliva.

You should be able to discuss the general maintenance of the tack in addition to the expectations for Stage 1. Further knowledge on oiling and storage of tack is expected. Consider the preparation of leather work (saddles and bridles) and synthetic materials (boot and some girths) before storing.

4. Know how to fit and remove tack needed for exercise

4.1–4.4

(If you have to wait for the assessor to come to talk to you and it is cold, it may be worth putting the horse's rug on over his saddle to help keep him warm.)

When discussing the fit of the tack things to consider are:

Bridle:

Is the width of the leather of the bridle a good size for the horse's head?

Is the browband too big/too small?

Are the buckles attached to the cheekpieces centrally positioned?

Is the bit wide enough? It should pull straight across the mouth and there be about one finger's width between the bit ring and the horse's lips.

Is the bit in the correct position in the mouth? The horse should be just 'smiling'.

Is the noseband the correct size?

Saddle:

There are numerous different types of saddle today.

The saddle should not look too big or too small on the horse.

The saddle must not rest on the loins.

All of the panels should touch the horse.

The saddle should be in balance on the horse's back.

There should be daylight through the gullet when the rider is mounted. The adage that you should be able to get a fist between the pommel and the withers is not agreed by everybody today. It depends on the make, design and style of the saddle.

4.5

There are a variety of ways to untack a horse. As long as the method chosen is safe for the horse, person and equipment then this is suitable.

If the weather is cold then the horse should be rugged-up as quickly as possible after removing the equipment.

4.6

When discussing the fit of the tack you may also be asked to discuss the safety of it. Ensure all the stitching is safe.

Make sure the holes for the buckles are not stretched or torn.

Check anywhere where leather and metal meet as this is a point of wear.

Check the general suppleness of the tack. Is it well maintained or could it do with a good clean?

Make sure the metal parts are not nickel. There are fewer and fewer nickel stirrups and bits around now. You can recognise them by their yellowy colour. They are prone to wear, bending and snapping so it is better to use stainless steel.

It is important to be aware of these factors because should the tack break when being used, an accident is likely to occur. If negligence can be proved a riding school may be sued in these circumstances.

When cleaning and checking tack any potential issues must be highlighted to the senior member of staff responsible.

5. Know relevant health and safety legislation

5.1

Consider good practice when working around the horse at all times, this to include:

Suitably securing the horse as required.

Safe handling and storage of equipment.

Reporting any changes of behaviour of the horse to a senior staff member.

Reporting and damaged equipment.

Only using appropriate equipment for which there has been appropriate training.

Unit 2a: The principles of horse health and anatomy

1. Know the horse's skeleton

1.1

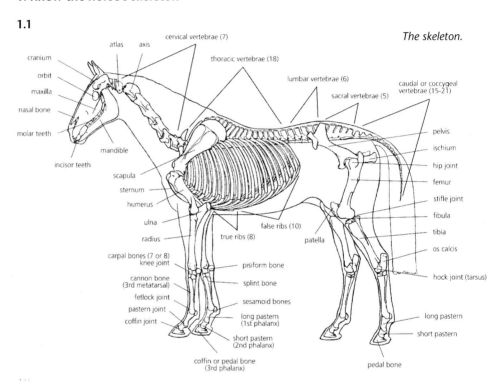

The skeleton.

2. Know the structure, function and potential problems of the horse's foot

2.1

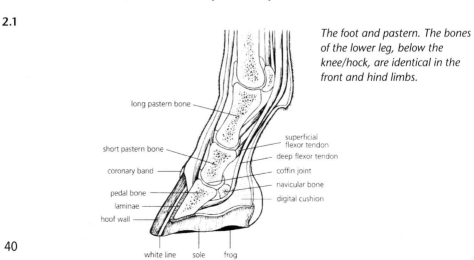

The foot and pastern. The bones of the lower leg, below the knee/hock, are identical in the front and hind limbs.

2.2

The foot has the following functions:

Distributes the horse's weight.

Expands each time it comes to the ground to help absorb concussion.

The concave shape of the sole and the wedge shape of the frog both help with grip.

The plantar cushion aids circulation and helps the blood flow back up the legs.

2.3

If a horse's feet are left and the toes grow too long this upsets the hoof/pastern axis and the balance of the foot.

This leads to the heels growing forward and becoming lower. Issues that can arise from this include:

Tendon strain.

Bruising.

Chronic heel pain.

Coffin joint inflammation.

Cracked heels.

Navicular syndrome.

3. Know the position of the horse's main internal organs

3.1

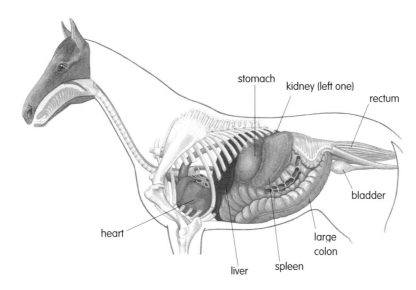

Major internal organs of the horse. Note that the lungs (not shown) lie within the ribcage.

41

4. Know the basic structure of the horse's digestive system

4.1–4.2
Basic structure of the horse's digestive system:
The alimentary canal is the whole digestive system from lips to anus.
The lips pick up the food.
The food is bitten with the incisor teeth.
The molar teeth masticate the food and it is mixed with saliva.
A bolus of food (a small ball) is formed.
The bolus is forced past the soft palate into the pharynx by the base of the tongue.
The muscular action of the pharynx pushes the bolus into the oesophagus.
The bolus is sent down the oesophagus by peristalsis (waves of constriction).
It passes through the cardiac sphincter muscle into the stomach. This muscle stops the horse from being able to be sick.
The stomach is a holding vat and is about the size of a rugby football.
A small amount of digestion starts in the stomach.
The food passes through the pyloric sphincter muscle into the small intestine.
The small intestine consists of the duodenum, the jejunum and the ileum.
Bile and pancreatic juice continue digestion of the food.
The food then passes into the large intestine where the majority of digestion takes place.
The large intestine consists of the caecum, large colon, small colon, rectum and anus.

4.3
Without roughage/fibre a horse's digestive system cannot do its work and so a horse would not be able to take the required nutrients from the food.

5. Know how to recognise a horse's health, welfare and condition

5.1
Normal Temperature, Pulse and Respiration Rates (TPR) at rest are:
Temperature 38 °Celsius/100.5 °Fahrenheit.
Pulse 36–42 beats per minute.
Respiration 8–12 breaths per minute.

5.2
Stance and bodily functions as indicators of health.
Stance:
A sound horse will stand with both forelegs on the ground without being too far in front or under his body. He may rest one hind leg or the other, but there is no problem with

that unless he always rests the same leg and is reluctant to put any weight on it. A horse who is 'pointing' one or both forelegs may be showing signs of laminitis or other form of discomfort in his forefeet.

Bodily function:
The horse's droppings should be round, slightly moist and break when they hit the ground. Hard, dry pellets may mean he is not drinking enough water or not eating enough roughage. Very sloppy green 'cowpats' are often seen in spring when the grass is too lush. A horse will normally pass droppings between 8 and 12 times a day.

5.3

You should know your horse's normal behaviour. Anything that changes from this may be a sign he is unwell e.g.:
Not eating and drinking as he usually does.
Not being interested in what is going on.
Not looking relaxed in his stable or, alternatively, seeming *too* quiet.
Signs of unusual sweating/rolling.
Nasal discharge.
Raised or lowered TPR.
Coat not shiny.
Looking 'tucked up'.

5.4

An *unsoundness* is any abnormality which interferes with a horse's usefulness. A *lameness* is an unsoundness that negatively affects a horse's way of going and should be seen by a vet. Signs include:
Standing awkwardly in his box.
Resting or 'pointing' a forefoot.
Heat or pain in legs or feet.
Irregular steps or strides when moving.
Generally foreleg lameness shows by the horse lifting his head when the lame foot hits the ground.
Generally when a horse is lame in a hind leg his head will nod down when the lame leg hits the ground. A dropped hip on one side may also be evidence of hind limb lameness.

5.5

A horse should have his teeth checked at least once a year. The lower jaw is narrower than the upper jaw and consequently the grinding action of the molars can lead to sharp edges on the outer edge of the upper jaw and the inner edges of the lower jaw.

Signs that the teeth may need rasping:
Hay dunking.
Abnormal chewing action.
Quidding (the horse dropping food as he eats).
Weight loss.
Long fibres in droppings.
Head-shy.
Reluctant to take the bit.
Unhappy in the mouth when being ridden.
Head-shaking.

6. Know how to recognise and treat minor wounds

6.1
Common types of wound are:
Puncture wound – small, but penetrating hole e.g. nail.
Incised/clean cut wound – e.g. glass, knife.
Tear wound – rough edges, e.g. barbed wire.
Bruised/contused wound – skin not broken e.g. kick.

6.2
Wound treatment:
Stop the bleeding.
Clean the wound thoroughly either by cold hosing or by using salty water and cotton wool.
If the wound is very small it may not need to be dressed. If a dressing is required antibiotic powder or spray is useful.
If the wound is bigger and the vet will be needed to deal with it then *do not put any form of powder or spray on it* prior to the vet's visit.
Always check the horse's tetanus cover is up to date.
A puncture wound may only look small, but it could be deep and the vet may need to give antibiotics.
If the horse needs time off work then the food must be adjusted accordingly.

6.3
The vet should be called to treat a wound in the following circumstances:
If the tetanus cover is not up to date.
If the wound needs stitching.

If the wound is pumping out bright red blood. (This will be from an artery: pressure will need to be applied to try to stem the bleeding.)

In any situation if you are at all unsure what to do.

7. Know how to care for sick horses

7.1

Principles of sick nursing:

Better for one person to look after the horse to reduce the chance of cross-contamination.

Follow all veterinary instructions closely.

Observe the horse regularly.

Keep the horse in a quiet environment. It may be necessary to isolate.

Keep the box dry and clean.

Box should be well ventilated.

A good thick bed that allows him to move about easily.

Warm, light rugs. Stable bandages if necessary.

Avoid bright lights shining at him if visiting at night.

Change water frequently.

Tempt with small quantities of palatable food at regular intervals.

Minimum grooming.

8. Know the importance of keeping horse records

8.1

It is important because it is unlikely that everything will be remembered. Some of the things that should be recorded are:

Vaccination dates.

Shoeing dates.

Dental records.

Worming records.

Work undertaken .

Whenever the vet was called and what the outcome was.

The owner can then get an all-round picture of what the horse is doing, when everything needs to be repeated and (for the riding school situation) how much the horse is earning, and the costs.

9. Know the importance of worming

9.1

All horses are likely to have a worm burden. It is necessary to keep worms to a minimum so the horse can thrive. A horse with a large worm burden may look unthrifty, be thin and have diarrhoea. He may well have frequent colic. An excessive worm burden can lead to death.

9.2

Many people worm their horses on a regular basis and change the type of wormer to try to stop a resistance to the drugs building up. Others now adopt a more scientific model and undertake faecal worm counts by collecting a sample of droppings and sending them away for analysis. The horses can then be wormed as necessary. This method is based on facts and can help save a horse owner money as the horse may not need to be wormed as frequently. This can also help to slow down a resistance to wormers.

You should know something of the general life-cycle of worms – specific worms are covered in greater depth in the later exams levels.

Unit 2b: The principles of shoeing, clipping and trimming horses

1. Know the reasons for clipping and relevant welfare issues
Although this is a 'principles' unit there is no substitute for clipping practice. This will help you to understand how to assemble clippers, how to clip and the issues involved. You will speak about this much better if you have a lot of practical experience.

1.1–1.2
Reasons for clipping and welfare implications are:
To enable the horse to work harder without distress.
Avoids sweating and so helps the horse to maintain condition.
The horse dries off quicker after work and so is less liable to catch a chill.
It is easier to keep him clean and tidy.
He looks smarter.
The first clip is usually in October and a horse should be re-clipped as often as necessary. It is not usual to clip after the end of January as this may have a detrimental effect on the summer coat that will be coming through.

1.3
Types of clip are shown in the accompanying pictures.

Full clip – this clip is usually only used for horses in consistent, very hard work: sometimes hunters are fully clipped for their first clip and then a hunter clip is used after that

Hunter clip – traditionally used for a horse that is hunting

Blanket clip – this is useful for horses working quite hard but also spending some time turned out

Chaser clip – this can be used for a horse in work that is likely to spend time standing around e.g. in a riding school

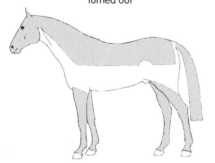

Trace clip – this can be used for ponies and horses spending some time out in a field as well as doing moderate work

Neck and belly clip – this is ideal for woolly ponies that do occasional work to stop them from sweating too much

2. Know how to assemble and maintain clippers

2.1

You may well be asked to put some clippers together. This is a task that candidates generally do very badly and it shows they do not have the required experience. The clipper blades come in pairs and there is usually a spring and a screw to attach them to the body of the clippers. Each make is different and you should ensure that you have practised with several different sets. Make sure that the larger flatter clipper blade is positioned so that it is the part that will touch the horse's skin. The spring and screw should come out of the top of the blades. If they are positioned the other way up you will not be able to clip as there will be a protrusion that will stop the blade from running smoothly along the horse's coat. Be careful not to lose the screw or spring. It may be better to assemble them over a table, so that if you drop one part it will be found easily. The manual for the clippers will tell you the tension at which the screw should be set.

2.2–2.3

Prior to clipping, check that there is a circuit-breaker in the electrical supply. Oil the clippers where indicated.

Get the horse used to the noise before starting. Start clipping on the shoulder and use long strokes, travelling against the lie of the hair.

Keep the clippers well-oiled and clean throughout the process. When checking the work you have done, turn the clippers off. This will help them to remain cooler. Do not let them overheat. Test the blades on the back of your hand occasionally. If they get hot then stop clipping. If the blades were newly sharpened they should easily do a full clip. Send the blades to be sharpened regularly. Have a spare pair available in case they start to become blunt whilst clipping.

2.4

The horse should be clean and dry. The clip you are going to do should be decided before you start. It is possible to mark the clip out on the horse (using tailor's chalk or saddle soap) to ensure the clip is level on both sides of the horse. The quicker and more efficient you are the less the horse will become fractious.

The clipping box should have good light. A rubber floor is the best surface, and some people give the horse a haynet. Others feel this discourages the horse from standing still. There should be a rug close to hand so that when clipping has finished the horse can be rugged up immediately.

The person who is clipping should wear a hard hat and rubber-soled footwear and be sure to keep the electrical flex out of the way. The assistant should be wearing hard hat and gloves and be observant.

It must be remembered that if we take off some of the horse's winter coat which is designed to help keep him warm in cold weather then we must put on extra rugs to compensate for this. A cold horse is not a happy horse and will require more feed to keep his condition. A horse should not be clipped just because the rider wants him to look 'nice'. A horse should only be clipped when his work load dictates this.

Most horses who are frightened of clipping have not been introduced to the clippers carefully enough. You may need to go back to the beginning to get them used to it.

3. Know why and how to pull manes and tails

3.1–3.3

This is done mainly for aesthetic/appearance reasons. A pulled mane is easier to plait and keep tidy. A pulled tail shows off the quarters, especially for showing.

Native ponies and those who live out all year should not be pulled. The mane and tail give protection against the elements.

Mane-pulling:
This is best done after exercise – the pores of the skin are open. It may well take several sessions if the mane is long and/or thick.
Use a metal mane comb (short teeth).
Backcomb a small amount of hair.
Pull out long hairs you are holding. You can pull them out with your fingers or twist round the comb and pull.
Do not pull out the hairs on top of the mane. They will re-grow and be spiky.

Tail-pulling:
Make sure the tail is well brushed out. Stand to the side of the horse's hindquarters.
Take a few hairs from the top underside of the tail.
Wrap round the comb and pull.
Do over a few days if necessary.

4. Know why and how to trim horses

4.1–4.4
This gives the horse a smarter appearance.
Use blunt-ended scissors and a mane comb.
Tail: get an assistant to put their arm under the top of the dock to lift the tail slightly. Trim the base of the tail to the level required. Show horses and hunters often have a tail that is short enough to show off the hocks or stop getting muddy. Trim as often as necessary.

Ears: do not trim inside the ears. Hold the sides of the ear together to close the ear and trim along this line, cutting off the protruding hair.

Coronary band: trim round the top of the coronary band making a straight, neat line, trimming the hair that grows down. Be careful not to damage the coronary band.

Mandible: the long hair under the chin can be trimmed or clipped off. A comb and scissors makes it look more natural.

Whiskers: some people cut off the long hairs around the eyes, and whiskers round the nose and mouth. This is not advisable as the horse uses them as sensory organs to limit injury.

Feathers: thick feathers can be clipped off, moving against the lie of the hair. Straggly feathers can be trimmed off using a comb and scissors.

You would not trim a horse who lives out all year round. Native ponies should not be trimmed as they are shown in their natural state.

5. Know the procedure for shoeing, including the use of farrier's tools

5.1
Horses are shod for protection. Some horses who only work on an artificial surface and/or grass may not need to be shod. They will need to have their feet trimmed though. Horses need to be shod every 4–6 weeks. Feet should be picked out at least twice a day.

5.2
The shoeing procedure is as follows:
Buffer and hammer are used to raise the clenches ready to remove the old shoe.
The pincers lever off the shoe – starting at the heel on one side, then the heel on the other and moving down the shoe quarter on one side then the other and then prising off at the toe.
Hoof-cutters cut off excess growth.
Drawing knife removes ragged sole and frog.
Foot is rasped level.
Space is cut for toe/quarter clips with drawing knife.
If hot shoeing, the shoe is forged.
The shoe is hammered on the anvil and a pritchel is hammered into a nail hole for carrying the shoe.
The shoe is carried to the foot and burnt on the horn to show any adjustments that need to be done.
Once it is the correct shape and size the shoe is immersed in cold water.
The shoe is nailed on. Usually a toe nail is put in first to stop the shoe slipping. The nails go between the white line and the outside of the hoof.
The nail ends are twisted off and they are rasped smooth.
A bed is made for the clenches.
Clenches are push down with a nail clencher or knocked down with a hammer with the pincers under the nail head.
The toe/quarter clips are tapped back.
The rasp is used to tidy up the foot.

5.3

A well-shod foot should have the clenches all in a line. A farrier will put in as many nails as necessary, but traditionally there are four nails in the outside of the foot and three on the inside. The shoe should fit the foot (unless it is a remedial shoe for a particular purpose). The hoof/pastern angle should not be broken. The heels should be supported by the shoe.

5.4

Be able to identify farriers' tools and know their uses.

6. Know the procedure for removing twisted shoe in an emergency

6.1

Place the foot between your legs if it is a front shoe. Alternatively, rest a hind leg on your thigh. Using the driving hammer and buffer, lift the clenches that are still in place. Then take the pincers and, starting at the heel, pull the shoe down and away from the foot: one heel then the other heel, then the quarter and the other quarter and finally the toe.

Unit 3a: The principles of watering, feeding and fittening horses

1. Know the rules of watering and understand their reasons

1.1 –1.2

A horse cannot maintain good health without good access to water to maintain his hydration status. This is just as important in the winter when access to water may be difficult if the source is frozen or limited.

A clean, constant supply of fresh water should always be available.

A horse's body is between 60–70 per cent water. Water is lost in a variety of ways from the body and so needs replacement. Horses drink between 38– 45 litres (8½–10 gallons) daily.

Water should be changed regularly – this avoids the build-up of ammonia.

All containers should be scrubbed regularly – encourages the horse to drink.

Do not allow a horse a long drink when he is very hot or straight after hard work – this can lead to colic. To prevent this give small amounts every 15 minutes.

Water before feeding – a slightly old-fashioned rule that came from when a horse did not have free access to water.

Horses should not be allowed to drink from sandy-bottomed streams as this can lead to sand being ingested and colic.

Troughs in fields must be checked daily.

If going to a competition it is advisable to take you own water to avoid the horse being put off from drinking.

1.3

Water can be provided in various ways and situations.

In a loosebox:

Buckets can be provided in the corner of a box with the handle turned towards the wall. A bucket clipped onto the wall puts the horse's head in an unnatural position for drinking. While this method is labour intensive, and there is the possibility of the bucket being knocked over, buckets are easy to clean and it is easy to monitor how much has been drunk. You can also administer medicine in water readily by this method.

Automatic waterers are labour-saving, and should ensure that horses are never without water (although unprotected pipes can freeze in winter). However, they can be difficult to clean and, unless they have meters fitted, you can't tell how much a horse is drinking. It is hard to administer medicine in water provided by this method.

In the field:

Troughs need to be cleaned and filled regularly (hosepipe is easiest, although a self-filling trough ensures constant supply). Troughs must have no sharp edges. Do not site near trees or field gate. In cold weather, ice needs to be broken at least twice a day.

Natural supplies may have drawbacks. Water in rivers/streams may be contaminated; the field may be prone to flooding; access may not be safe. Pond water is likely to be stagnant so ponds should be fenced off.

In fields, buckets should be used only as a last resort. They are hard work to carry and easily knocked over, and will freeze very easily in winter.

2. Know the rules of feeding and understand their reasons

2.1–2.2

Feed according to: work, bodyweight, type, temperament, age, time of year, rider's abilities. It is important to remember that every horse is an individual. The amount and type of food given must be related to the above factors. Horses who are not fed enough will lose condition and will not be able to perform. Horses who are overfed can become troublesome, prone to filled legs, joint issues, digestive disorders, laminitis and obesity.

Feed little and often. The horse's stomach is the size of a rugby ball. Feeding little and often mimics what he would do in the wild. It helps to keep the digestive system working and helps keep him occupied. It also means he is kept occupied for longer and consequently will be happier.

Feed plenty of roughage/fibre. Without this the digestive system is unable to work. It also helps to mimic his natural eating habits.

Always feed good-quality forage. Poor-quality, cheap food is false economy. The horse may not eat it. If he does it may lead to colic or respiratory disorders.

Keep to a regular routine. Horses are creatures of habit and thrive on routine.

Make changes of food gradually. 'Food type bacteria' in the horse's gut break down the food. If a sudden change is made there may not be enough bacteria to break down the new food and this could lead to colic. Changing food type slowly enables the new bacteria to be built up.

Feed at least one hour before exercise. A full stomach will press on the diaphragm and impede breathing.

Do not feed straight after exercise. During exercise blood is pushed to the muscles away from the digestive organs. This means that nutrients will not be removed and transported round the body so efficiently until metabolism has returned to normal.

Feed something succulent every day. Food such as apples and carrots can provide vitamins and minerals and are enjoyed by horses.

Keep all utensils and equipment clean. This ensures food is not contaminated and remains appealing to the horse.

A clean, constant supply of fresh water should always be available.

3. Know a variety of feedstuffs, their preparation and suitability for horses

3.1
All food given should be of highest quality, good colour, dry, smell pleasant, be free from dust and mould. There should be no weeds or poisonous plants in forage.
You will be expected to identify the feed samples and comment on the quality, colour, smell, etc.
You should be able to discuss the preparation of bran mash and sugar beet.

3.2
Identifying heating or fattening foodstuffs.

Heating feedstuffs include:
Maize, oats, barley, peas and beans.
Some specific compound feeds (competition mix, racehorse mix/cubes, etc.)

Fattening feedstuffs include:
Barley, linseed, some compound feeds (conditioning mix/cubes). Including oils (lipids) in the feed can be useful, but potentially fattening if fed in quantity.

3.3
When identifying feedstuffs suitable for a variety of horses be mindful that, while most are potentially suitable, selection is often based on quality and whether fed as a straight or as compound (you must read the label on the bag to determine suitability of a mix/cube).
You should know the difference in feeding a variety of types of horses, e.g. old and sick horses; grass-kept horse or pony.

4. Know about feeding bulk food

There are two basic types of hay.

Meadow hay is from mixed pasture fields that have been allowed to grow. Feeding value varies greatly.

Seed hay is from fields that have been sown specifically for hay. The feeding value is higher than meadow hay. The crop tends to be coarser.

4.1

Soaking hay reduces the dust and fungal spores that may be ingested by the horse. Soaking hay for 5 minutes reduces the number of particles by 97 per cent. Soaking for several hours shows significant loss of nutrients. Do not re-use water in which hay has been soaked.

Steaming hay is a good alternative. There is less loss of nutrients and very little water is used.

4.2

Haylage is an alternative to hay. It is about 50 per cent wet matter and is baled and wrapped in plastic. Different forms, with differing nutritional values are now available, but it usually has a higher feeding value than hay and many horses work quite hard on it without any hard feed. Damaged bales may be unusable, not only because the feed value is compromised, but because of the possibility of health risks.

Silage is generally considered unsuitable to feed to horses as the water content is high and it can be prone to infection by botulism.

Grass nuts can be used as part of the bulk content. They are useful in summer when there is little grass or hay.

Good-quality oat straw is sometimes used as bulk. It has a low feeding value and condition of horses needs monitoring carefully.

5. Know how to produce a feed chart

5.1

A feed chart is essential to ensure each horse is fed the correct amount of suitable food. Any trained member of staff can then feed the horses.

5.2

To make a feed chart, use a black or white board. The horse's names are listed and the number of times a day they are fed and what they are given are written on the board. Supplements and medication should be noted. If there is not a white or black board then a book could be used, but this could become untidy very quickly.

6. Know how to get a turned away horse fit for non-stressful exercise up to one and a half hours a day

6.1–6.3

It takes 6–8 weeks to get a horse fit for non-stressful exercise. This is based on working the horse six days a week with one day off.

Week before programme starts:

Bring horse in daily.

Give handful of hard feed.

Check tack still fits.

Get horse shod.

Check vaccinations, teeth and worming.

Start grooming and tidying up.

Use a well-ventilated box to help reduce the likelihood of coughs.

Week one:

Walking exercise only all week.

Start with about 15 minutes on day one and build up about an hour by the end of the week.

Use a sound, flat surface e.g. the road. Rutted ground can cause tendon, ligament and joint issues. An outdoor artificial surface could be used initially should the horse's behaviour be suspect. Walking on roads helps harden tendons and tone muscles. Watch for rubs and galls.

At this stage the horse may still be receiving 100 per cent bulk feed depending on temperament and attitude. If he is receiving hard feed it may be only up to 10 per cent of his total feed. A pre-prepared mix or cube is best as it provides a complete balanced diet.

Week two:

Walking exercise only.

By the end of the second week the horse should be walking for the length of time he will be working each day – for this programme about 1 ½ hours. Start hill work in walk by the end of the week. This makes the horse work harder without any more stress on the forelegs.

Feed may still be 100 per cent bulk, but can begin to change to 10 per cent hard feed and 90 per cent bulk.

Week three:

Introduce trot work in short sessions several times during the 1½-hour period. This should be a balanced working trot. Do not overstress the horse.

Feed may now be 15 per cent hard feed and 85 per cent bulk.

57

Week four:

Increase trot work progressively.; start trotting uphill. Work on grass can start if this has not started already. The first four weeks will have lasting benefits to the muscles, tendons and ligaments. It should not be cut short.

Feed may still be based on 15 per cent hard feed, but a little more hard feed may be necessary depending on the type and build of the individual horse.

Week five:

Introduce short sessions of canter, building up the length of time as per trot work. Lungeing can be introduced. Basic schooling can start with big school figures and trotting poles.

Feed may still be based on 15 per cent hard feed.

Week six:

Increase length of canters. Start hill work in canter towards the end of the week. Schooling becoming a little more intense. Small showjumps and natural obstacles can be utilised. Maybe enter a small dressage competition at the end of the week.

Feed may now need about 20 per cent hard feed.

Week seven:

Continue the work as per week six. Schooling for longer, with smaller (more demanding) figures. Canter for longer and faster if required. Showjumping/hunter trials competition.

Feed may still be based on 20 per cent, or the horse may need a little more.

Week eight:

If the fitness is improving then continue in the same manner. If not, then increase the intensity of the work.

Only feed more hard feed if the horse is not coping with the work.

6.4

Possible causes of leg injuries.

Concussive injuries can be caused by hard ground, riding too fast on poor going/hard ground conditions, trotting in an unbalanced way on roads.

Strain injuries can be caused by jumping on deep or uneven going, riding downhill at speed, poor riding unbalancing the horse, too much work when horse not fit enough.

6.5

As the horse becomes fitter his behaviour may change. He may become more tense and 'on his toes'. Do not overfeed him: always keep exercise ahead of feed. Make sure he spends time in the field to wind down. If his condition and the weather permit, then he can still live out. He only needs to be stabled if the work/weather prohibit his work.

If he is ridden on his own he may become 'nappy' in his behaviour. This is when he may not wish to leave the yard; he may walk slowly when leaving the yard and quickly (or be jogging) on return. This can then develop into not going forward and possible refusal to move, rearing or spinning back to the yard. To prevent this the horse should always be ridden positively forwards and if he shows such negative tendencies it may be useful to ride him in company to limit this behaviour.

When ridden in company as he gets fitter he may become more excitable and be inclined to jog. If this behaviour is allowed to develop he may be inclined to buck and leap about in the yard once moving forwards. To manage this, try to place him at the front of the other horses and ride forwards. It may be easier to mount him last in the group to avoid any unnecessary standing about and possible boredom developing.

7. Know how to care for a horse after work

7.1

Cooling off is important to give the horse's metabolism a chance to return to normal. It reduces stress. Injuries spotted early can be kept minimal.

Walk the horse (mounted or in hand) and allow him to stretch. If weather is cold a light rug may be needed. Once he stops blowing and has dried off, offer a small amount of water. Wash down. Dry off. Walk again. Offer more water. Check for injuries.

7.2

Once completely cooled down and no longer thirsty, the horse can be allowed to graze or be given a haynet The horse should have returned to 'normal' before offering hard feed.

The following day, check for knocks, cuts or swellings – these may become obvious once the horse has completely rested, or the day after competing.

Observe eating and behaviour and trot up for lameness (check for stiffness).

8. Know how to 'rough off' a horse

8.1

The process of getting a fit horse ready for turning out/holiday takes 10 –14 days. Over this period:

Amount of work is gradually cut down.

Amount of time spent in the field daily goes up.

Number of rugs is reduced.

Hard feed decreases.

Grooming is cut down.

Shoes may be taken off at the end of the period.

Turn out completely on a sunny day. Check him daily.

Unit 3b: The principles of stabling and grassland care for horses

1. Know the requirements for stable design and construction

1.1

Traditional stables are side by side in a yard and American barn stables are indoors usually either side of a central corridor. Some farm buildings can be converted to stabling and therefore may not have a traditional design.
Recommended sizes for purpose-built boxes are:
10ft x 10ft (3m x 3m) for a pony.
12ft x 12ft (3.6m x 3.6m) for a horse.
12ft x 14ft (3.6m x 4.2m) for a horse larger than 16.2hh.

Boxes for specialist use such as box-rested horses, stallions and foaling may be considerably bigger than standard.
Advantages and disadvantages of the American barn system.

Advantages:
Everything under one roof.
Security better.
They may be warmer than traditional stables in winter, particularly if made from modern thermally efficient materials.

Disadvantages:
If the central corridor is not wide enough, horses can be bullied.
Horses may be threatened by neighbours. (Although this can also happen in some conventional stables and the likelihood depends to an extent on the construction of walls between.)
Disease can travel more easily.
Ventilation may not be good enough.

1.2

There are a variety of materials used for stable construction.
Brick is fireproof, long-lasting, warm in winter, cool in summer. Brick stables are very expensive and can take a long time to construct.

Wood is popular, cheaper than brick, can be constructed in a day as long as the base is ready. Can be a fire hazard and needs regular maintenance. Horses can kick and chew wooden stables.

Breeze blocks are cheaper than brick, and fireproof. They take longer to construct than wooden stables, are not aesthetically pleasing and can be cold in winter. Also, they may not be as robust and secure as brick, and can be compromised by a large horse prone to kicking or leaning on the stable walls.

Corrugated iron has edges that become defined over time and can lead to injury. It's not strong and can be kicked through. If this occurs then the broken edges can cause injury to the horse. Very hot in summer, very cold in winter, this is generally an old-fashoined material and not ideal for use in stables.

The stable roof needs to be high enough– about 12 ft (3.6m) to the eaves – so the horse will not hit his head. A pitched roof increases the air volume and circulation within the stable as well as helping the rain to run off the roof efficiently. Guttering is necessary to collect rain.
Various materials are used for roofing:
Tiles are expensive. Need good maintenance to ensure that loose tiles are repaired.

Wood is usually covered in roofing felt to make it waterproof. This requires maintenance – felt can be ripped by the wind. No natural light comes through the roof so the stable is often dark.

Corrugated iron is noisy, lacks insulation. More acceptable if fitted over a wooden roof but again, this makes the stable dark.

Onduline is similar to corrugated iron, but coated and so insulated. Plastic sheets can be inserted to give some natural light.

1.3
Ventilation is important to provide clean, fresh air and help disperse stable odours arising from urine, etc. However, draughts are undesirable.
Traditional stables usually have the window on the same wall as the door to stop through draughts. The windows should open inwards and be protected. Louvre boards or air bricks near the eaves enhance air flow. Craw chimneys on the ridge of the roof also help circulation.
Ventilation in barn systems can be limited depending upon the pitch of the roof and any vents within the roof. if the roofing system and ventilation are poor then fans can be incorporated to aid the air circulation and temperature control.

1.4

Drainage is important in the stable so that the horse does not stand in any urine, and to aid washing down, and in the yard so that it is kept clean and 'pooling' does not occur. The stable floor should slope to help avoid this. In many stables, the slope is from front to back, with a drainage channel along back wall with a drainage hole in the middle of the wall. Be prepared to comment on the drainage, as some systems (particularly in American barns) may slope from back to front with drains in the centre or side of the main stable aisle.

1.5

As few fixture and fittings as possible are desirable for the horse's safety. A tie-ring at about 1.5m (5 ft). A ring for a haynet – minimum height about 2m (6ft 6in). If a mineral lick holder is on the wall it must have a lick in it or the edges can be dangerous. A manger is not necessary – it takes up room, is difficult to clean and is at an unnatural height for feeding. Some means of providing water is essential (see **Unit 3a, 1.3**). An electric light is necessary; the light itself must be protected and the switch out of the horse's reach.

2. Know about horse behaviour and welfare when stabled

2.1

Living in a stable takes away freedom to move, eat and interact with other horses when they want to. It may lead to repetitive habits, being unhappy, or difficult behaviour in some horses, although others may adapt easily.
Turning out regularly, *ad lib* bulk food, being ridden regularly and being able to see other horses will help.

2.2

A new horse in the yard:
Some people put in a quarantine area for two weeks.
May be nervous/unsure – take extra care.
Stable bandages/brushing boots may help prevent injury.
Needs a regular routine.
Preferable if he can see other horses – a quiet one is ideal, and will help to set an example.
Preferable to have the same person to look after him – can monitor behaviour more closely and ensure horse is eating and drinking.

2.3

Signs of nervousness/undesirable behaviour:

Ears set flat back.

Staring, focused eye.

Head in the corner/quarters towards humans.

Tail twitching/held high/clamped down.

Body tense.

Agitated.

Sweating/frequent droppings.

2.4

When handling a nervous horse, bear the following in mind:

Needs to learn to trust.

Needs consistent behaviour/regular routine.

So be fair and use consistent discipline.

Tie up horse when working in stable.

Wear a riding hat/safe footwear; gloves for leading.

Be observant.

Relax/breathe/talk to the horse.

3. Know the requirements for grassland care and pasture maintenance

3.1

Suitable acreage is two acres for first horse and one acre for each horse after that.

Safe fencing – ideal is post and rail with a hedge behind.

Self-filling water trough away from the gate or trees.

Secure gate.

Shelter of some sort.

Check daily for hazards like rabbit holes, litter.

No poisonous plants.

3.2

To maintain good-quality grazing:

Do not overgraze.

Rest regularly.

Employ cross-grazing with sheep or cattle.

Dig up weeds.

Pick up droppings daily.

Roll and harrow in spring.

Soil analysis is useful prior to fertilising to determine what type to use.

Fertiliser is often applied in spring (although some fertilisers applied in autumn). Keep horses off until washed in.

3.3

Poisonous plants.

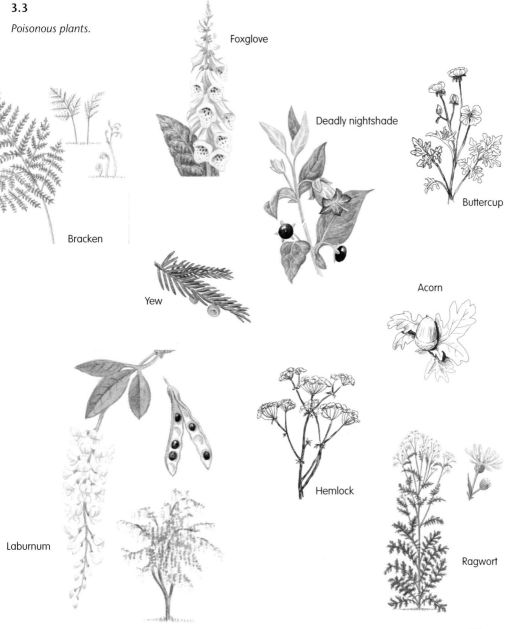

Foxglove

Deadly nightshade

Buttercup

Bracken

Yew

Acorn

Laburnum

Hemlock

Ragwort

4. Know about horse behaviour and welfare when at grass

4.1

Signs of an unsettled/unhappy horse are the same as for stabled horse.

A group in a field should be relaxed and content. If frightened by something they will run away from it. When they feel they are safe they will turn and look at the object and probably snort.

In summer horses may be annoyed by flies and biting insects. It may also be too hot for them – turn out at night and bring in during the day.

If grass is sparse and the ground hard, unshod horses may become footsore. They may also be hungry and so become fractious.

Mares and geldings are better kept in separate fields.

4.2

Horses may be difficult to catch for the following reasons:

They do not go out in the field often.

They know they are going to work – make sure there is a positive reason for coming in.

They may have been chastised previously when caught.

They don't trust the person catching them.

This can take time and patience to overcome. Turing out with other horses who are easy to catch could help. Leaving a well-fitting leather headcollar on could assist. If you have time, sit down or stand very still and let the horse come to you.

Unit 4: Lunge a horse under supervision

Although you can learn the theory of lungeing there is no substitute for practice. Lungeing in all stage exams is often weak. It is essential that you are proficient using the equipment and feel competent to lunge a horse you do not know.

1. Be able to lunge a horse

1.1
The lunge area will usually be an artificial surface. Make sure the area is safe. Take the weather conditions into account. If there is more than one horse being lunged in an area be aware of the other horse's behaviour. The surface should be marked out into areas and you need to stay within the area you are allocated.

1.2
You must wear a riding hat (done up) that conforms to current standards, gloves and boots (short boots and half chaps are suitable). Do not wear spurs.

1.3
You will be presented with a horse with a saddle and bridle on and you will be asked to fit the cavesson, side reins and make sure the rest of the tack is safe. Make sure the bridle noseband is removed if it interferes with the lunge cavesson.
The cavesson should:
* Be high enough so it doesn't pinch the lips.
* Be low enough so it doesn't rub the protruding cheek bone.
* Fit either under or over the cheek straps depending on its position. The noseband should be under the cheek straps.
* Fit snugly so it will not pull round into the horse's eye on the outside.
* Have the lunge line attached to the centre ring.

The stirrups should be fixed so they do not slip down.

Stirrups secured for lungeing so they will not slip down during exercise.

The side-reins should be attached to the girth strap so they do not slip down. The approximate length for the side-reins should be checked without attaching them to the bit. They should then be crossed at the withers and attached to the D ring.

Horse should have boots all round.

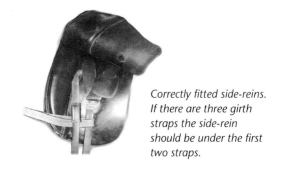

Correctly fitted side-reins. If there are three girth straps the side-rein should be under the first two straps.

1.4 – 1.5

Keep the whip under your arm behind you.

Make sure the lunge line is not twisted. It is acceptable as long as it is safe (but not with a lively horse) to put the lunge line on the floor to sort out. Make sure you are between the horse and the line. Be quick and efficient in taking it back up.

Send the horse out and make a triangle with the horse as the base and you as the apex. Make sure your voice and body language are positive. Upward transitions in a bright voice, downward in a lower, more soothing voice.

To change the rein, halt the horse on the circle. Change your line hand and put the whip into your armpit so it is behind you. Reel yourself out to the horse without taking your hand off the line. Pat him on the neck. Go to the other side, bring the whip round behind you and send him out again. As long as you are efficient with the whip there is no need to pick up the lash.

Lunge on both reins. If the horse is going forward then attach the side-reins.

Do several transitions and changes of rein.

If you have a backward-thinking horse who knows how long the lunge whip is you may need to walk a circle with him to ensure he goes forward. If you need to use the lunge whip then aim to push the horse forward in the area of the second

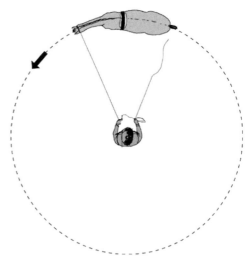

Good positioning of lunger in relation to the horse: handler in centre of circle; horse 'held' in a triangle between the lunge rein and the handler's whip and voice.

thigh. It is permissible to use the whip on the horse if it is necessary. Do not use the whip like a circus whip.

If you have a sensitive horse you may need to stand still on the circle and make sure your body language is not intimidating. The whip would need to be still and not threatening. You must respond to the horse's way of going to work towards a good rhythm that is correct for him.

1.6
When finished you will be asked to take the cavesson and side-reins off. This is to show efficiency and to allow the next candidate to then fit the equipment onto the horse before they lunge him.

2. Be able to work safely

2.1
At all times, remain in control of the horse and your equipment.

Be able to handle the lunge line and whip safely, practise changing the rein as this is often where things become muddled.

This includes whip control; cracking the whip is not good practice as may upset other horses working near you.

Lunge the horse according to the ground and weather conditions.

You should be able to develop an empathy with the horse and relate the work to his reactions and way of going.

3. Know how to lunge horses

3.1
Reasons for lungeing as a replacement for ridden exercise:

To exercise a horse who is sound enough to lunge, but cannot be ridden for some reason.

To train a young horse to prepare for backing.

To build up muscle tone.

To improve suppleness.

To help retain a badly trained horse.

To get rid of excess energy.

To start a horse over poles.

To give variety within a programme.

3.2

Procedures associated with lungeing horses:

Check the horse's tack and equipment.

Warm up the horse for 5 minutes in walk, trot and maybe canter. This to be carried out on both reins.

The side-reins can then be attached (they should have been previously fitted for the horse). Consider the size of the circle, ideally 15 m or larger.

Can warm the horse down by detaching the side-reins and allowing the horse to stretch whilst quietly walking a couple of circles.

3.3

Equipment and protective clothing when lungeing.

For the horse:

Bridle and saddle/roller.

Lungeing cavesson.

Side-reins.

Brushing boots, including overreach if required.

For the rider:

Hat – protects the head from bangs or possible kicks.

Sensible boots with heel (heel provides a grip if the horse pulls away).

Gloves – protects the hands from rope burns.

Breeches or comfortable-fitting trousers.

Lunge line, lunge whip.

3.4

Conditions which may affect lungeing.

Weather:

Hot – horse may be lazy and lethargic.

Cold – horse may be fresh or sharp.

Windy – Horse may be fresh and behave nervously.

Raining – horse may be miserable.

Surface:

Slippery – unexpected behaviour from the horse appearing insecure, and susceptible to knocks and injury.

Deep – horse may tire and can be susceptible to strains and injury.

Uneven – loss of rhythm, horse may stumble and lose balance.

You should also be aware and take account of other horses in or nearby the arena.

3.5

Lungeing can be used for exercise or training.

Usually lasts for 20–30 minutes.

Ideally starts by warming up in walk and then trot on a large (15m plus) circle.

If the horse is sufficiently balanced then canter can be introduced.

Side-reins can be attached once the horse is warmed up and is going freely forward.

Dealing with problems:

Lunge line becomes muddled – learn to coil and uncoil the line, particularly when changing the rein (direction). Problems usually arise when there is a lack of practice in this skill.

Horse won't go forward – check body language, voice projection and authority. Use the lunge whip towards the hock to send the horse forward. Move with the horse to keep him moving forwards.

Horse falling in on circle – horse not going forward – see comment above.

Horse refusing to stop – if at the beginning of the section the horse is probably fresh. Use steady tweaks on the line to get the horse's attention.

Horse turning on the person lungeing – stay positioned more towards the horse's hip and keep working the horse forward.

4. Know the current health and safety legislation

4.1

Wear correct clothing.

Check arena for safety, footing and security of the area – gates.

Check that the tack is safe and suitably fitted – check boots and girth.

Organise lunge line and whip.

Position yourself towards the horse's shoulder before sending the horse out – avoid being close to the hindquarters.

If anyone else is having a problem in the school return to walk until the situation is safe and under control.

Stage 3 Revision Notes

Unit 1: Fit tack and equipment and care for the competition horse

1. Be able to work safely and efficiently

1.1–1.3
Remember:
Tie up the horse.
Skip out.
Keep equipment safe.
Keep work area tidy.
Work practically and efficiently.

2. Be able to put on and fit tack and boots for competition

2.1
Procedure for putting on and fitting a double bridle:
Take leather out of keepers and check approximate size against the horse's head.
Put headcollar round horse's neck with rope slipped through tie string.
Make sure bridoon is over the Weymouth.
Keep noseband out of horse's mouth whilst putting bridle on.
The bridoon bit should be a little higher than a normal snaffle and the Weymouth underneath it.
Put leather back in the keepers; do up the throat lash and noseband.
The curb chain fly link should lie so it slips through onto the lip strap and lies flat. The curb chain should do up under the bridoon and be twisted flat. It should lie in the curb groove and come into action when the Weymouth shank is at an angle of 45 degrees. Do not put the headcollar over the double bridle. Stand and hold the horse until the assessor comes.
You may be asked to fit a running martingale onto the same bridle. Put the martingale rings through the bridoon rein.

2.2

Fit the numnah, saddle and boots first in order that the horse can be tied up with the headcollar, then fit the bridle to avoid the horse having to stand with the headcollar over the double bridle.

Discuss the use of the specialist boots and type of saddle chosen – fit and design.

3. Know and understand how to fit tack for competition

3.1

Justify fit.

You must know how to, and be able to discuss, the fit and use of tack for competition, including the double bridle. For example:

Various nosebands – including those for specialist competition use – Grakle, etc.

Competition saddles – dressage, jumping, girths, overgirths, martingales and breastplates.

Boots and bandages for all disciplines, and when they are not permitted.

Know when the equipment can and cannot be used regarding the discipline rules.

3.2

Discuss the influence of poor tack to include the effect on the horse (head-tossing, influence on the outline, changes of behaviour, not going forwards and napping, sores and rubs).

3.3

Studs may be used in front or back shoes. Some people only put one on the outside of each shoe to lessen the possibility of catching the opposite leg. Others put two studs in each foot to help maintain the foot balance. Road studs are permanent small studs, but they can upset the foot balance. Pointed studs are for hard ground, bull-nosed studs for soft going. Once they are finished with, studs should be unscrewed and the holes plugged with cotton wool.

4. Know and understand the action of a variety of bits in general use for competition

4.1

When fitting a bit every horse is an individual. Any bit is only as good as the hands at the end of the reins. Bits can be split into several families:

Snaffles include loose ring, eggbutt, double-jointed, branded bits such as KK, Neue Schule including the bridoon.

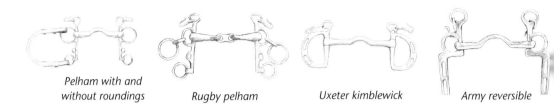

Pelham with and without roundings   *Rugby pelham*   *Uxeter kimblewick*   *Army reversible*

Curbs include the Weymouth.

Pelham family

Gags – Cheltenham, American, three-ring.

There is also a group of specialist bitless bridles – hackamores, etc.

Gag snaffle on horse's head with two reins

Bitless bridle

4.2

Bits can apply pressure to the:

Poll.

Tongue.

Bars.

Lips/corners.

Nose.

Chin groove.

Roof of the mouth.

Hackamore

You should be able to discuss the action of the bits on these pressure points.

5. Be able to select and put on exercise/schooling bandages

5.1

Exercise bandages are used for support and protection. When selecting, remember that a tail bandage is 7.5cm (3 in) wide and an exercise bandage is 10cm (4 in) wide.

Exercise bandages must not impede flexion of the joints nor be too tight. You should be able to get a finger between the padding and the leg. Bandaging too tightly can damage blood supply, tendons and ligaments. Horse can become used to the support they give.

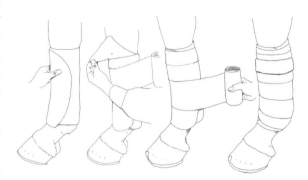

Exercise bandages

Fybagee/Gamgee should be correct size: wrap round leg from front to back.

Put bandage on from front to back.

Leave a spare tab at the beginning of the bandage that can be turned down after first wrap round the leg.

Cover two-thirds of the bandage each time.

Bandage down as far as the ergot; make an inverted 'V' with the bandage at the front of the leg.

Ties must not be tighter than the bandage.

Use a reef knot/bow for the ties and fold down the bandage over the knot.

Tape or sew for security.

Polo wraps are becoming more popular for exercise. They do not require padding and are often applied so they go under the fetlock.

6. Know and understand why exercise/schooling bandages are used

6.1

Bandaging is to help support and/or protect the tendons and ligaments of the lower leg. It protects from knocks from the other leg, or a fence.

There is some debate on the influence on correct bandaging, correct tension, slippage, overheating (of boots too). The reasons why bandaging may not be used are often related to an individual not being able to bandage correctly, the difficulty in applying a suitable tension, or increased heat to the lower limb and so boots may be fitted instead.

6.2

Bandages are only as good as the application and fit. They can slip, give uneven pressure causing damage to the soft tissues, or even come undone.

7. Know and understand how to care for a horse after competition

7.1–7.3

Cooling down a horse following competition or strenuous exercise is important for horse's physical and mental well-being.

Cool down by walking with a loosened girth and noseband. Walk until the horse stops blowing – pulse and respiration rates will come back down. Blood and oxygen will keep flowing.

May need to fit a cooler rug if weather is cold.

Untack horse when dry.

Wash down and walk dry again.

Offer small drinks every 10 minutes.

Allow the horse to nibble grass (haynet if suitable).

Check for injuries/trot up for soundness.

Give hard feed and haynet when horse back in stable.

Check that he looks happy/content.

Next day, check for injuries/trot up for lameness.

Feed as normal.

Turn out or walking exercise.

8. Know the procedures, legislative requirements and qualifications for travelling horses to and from competition

8.1

Check vehicle for:

Fuel, lights, oil, brakes, tyre pressure, paperwork up to date. Know the route/have map in cab.

Check security of floor and put bedding on floor.

Check for good ventilation.

If the vehicle is a trailer then check tow hitch.

Position vehicle safely.

8.2

It is sensible to have a list of what is required and tick the items off. Suggested items: horse's passport, tack, grooming kit, water, buckets, sponges, sweat scraper, first aid kits, rugs, studs and spanner, food and drink, riding clothes.

Dress horse as required – leather headcollar, poll guard, boots/bandages, tail bandage/tail guard, rug – depending on weather conditions.

8.3

When loading and unloading, safety is paramount. Wear gloves and hard hat.

Loading:

Make sure everybody knows what they are doing and where to stand.

If the horse is unknown or difficult, put a bridle on over the headcollar.

Lead the horse positively to the ramp – do not look at him.

He goes up the middle of the ramp, the leader slightly to the side.

Assistant closes the partition. Possibly give a reward. Tie the horse up.

If loading into a trailer and there is only one horse, put him in the offside compartment to help balance the camber of the road.

Drive as smoothly as possible. Try not to brake quickly. A smooth journey will make it more likely that the horse will load well in the future.

Unloading:

The area must be safe, with enough room for ramp and horse to come down.

The ramp should be as flat as possible.

Go into the vehicle and untie the horse before the partition is opened.

Assistant opens partition. Lead horse straight down the middle of the ramp.

Do not turn while the horse's hind legs still on ramp.

8.4

When loading difficult horses, practice makes perfect. Teach a horse to load before you need to travel.

Try to decide why the horse will not load – is he frightened, or naughty?

Have control of the horse with a bridle.

Position vehicle so a wall creates a barrier on one side.

Shavings/straw on the ramp may make it more inviting.

Be positive but not aggressive.

If the horse stops at the bottom of the ramp get an experienced assistant who is wearing suitable personal protection to lift one forefoot then the other onto the ramp.

Use a bowl of nuts to encourage the horse up.

Lunge lines behind his quarters may help.

Take time and allow the horse to trust you. If you try to rush or get angry the whole thing will fall apart.

Unit 2: Horse health, anatomy and physiology

1. Be able to recognise good and bad conformation

1.1
Conformation is dictated by the bone structure of the horse. The way in which a horse is put together impacts on his way of going and soundness.
Should look in proportion.

2. Understand how conformation may affect a horse's way of going

2.1
Start at the head and go through the different parts of the body.

Head – should be in proportion to the rest of the horse. Should be set on well leaving room to flex.

Ears – relaxed, mobile and a good size.

Eyes – set wide apart. Kind expression. Good size.

Nostrils – big and wide for efficient intake of air.

Mouth/jaw – not parrot-mouthed or undershot. Big enough to take a bit comfortably.

Neck – in proportion to the rest of the body. Should appear to come up out of withers. If neck is too up out of withers may have issues becoming genuinely round in outline. Muscular topline. Sternocephalicus muscle under neck should not be pronounced – this usually means the horse carries his head too high. This may be a conformational issue or a developmental one from poor riding.

Shoulder – slope between 45 and 50 degrees. Upright shoulder can lead to short, choppy strides.

Chest – plenty of room for heart. Not too wide as this can lead to 'roll' in the canter. Not too narrow – forelegs may be too close, and brush.

Forelegs – looking from the front they should be straight from top of leg to middle of foot. Seen from the side, forearm and cannon bone should be in straight line. Good bone (circumference of leg below the knee). Large, flat knees. Not back at the knee, or tied in below the knee. Being over at knee may be acceptable for older horse, and some experienced competition riders do not see at as an issue. Cannon bones short and strong. Fetlocks large and flat. Pasterns not too sloping (which can lead to tendon strain) nor too upright (can lead to concussion). Fetlock angle should match the shoulder angle. Hoof/pastern axis should have a straight line.

Feet should be as near a pair as possible: not boxy or flat feet.

Withers – not too prominent or saddle fitting may be difficult.

Back – in proportion to rest of body. Too long a back is a potential weakness, although may prove supple and, in a brood mare, gives room for carrying the foal. A short back is strong, but may give a stiffer ride. Good depth of rib – heart and lung room. Loins should be broad and muscular.

Hind legs – seen from behind there should be a straight line from point of buttock, through hock and middle of foot. From the side there should be a straight line from point of buttock, point of hock down back of cannon bone to ground. Quarters should appear strong and well-muscled. Hocks should be large and 'well let down' (length from point of hock to fetlock appears short). Hind pasterns should slope at 50 –55 degrees. Hind feet more oval than front as designed to assist with pushing function of hind leg.

Tail – well set on.

2.2

The 'trotting up' procedure is used to assess action and lameness.

Look at the horse in the stable to see how he is standing – this could help to indicate if he is lame. Compare the legs for heat and lumps and bumps.

Put on a bridle.

If possible watch the horse as he moves out of the stable – stiffness might show.

Trot up on a firm, level surface.

The person leading the horse should walk away positively staying at the horse's shoulder leaving the head free, not looking back at him and not blocking him with their body. Turn the horse clockwise (away from the leader) and trot forwards positively, not dragging the horse and leaving the head free.

Watch the horse from front, back and side and when being turned.

2.3

In normal gaits the horse moves straight (hind legs following in tracks made by forelegs) and has a desire to go forward.

Faulty action includes: dishing, plaiting, brushing, daisy cutting.

2.4

If the horse is lame in walk do not trot him up.

If lame in front the horse's head will raise as the lame leg comes to the ground.

If lame in both forelegs the stride will be short.

Lameness behind is more difficult to recognise. The hip which goes up and down more is the lame leg. Look from the side also and see if the strides are level and the toes lifting off the ground equally.

3. Be able to locate the main superficial muscles

3.1

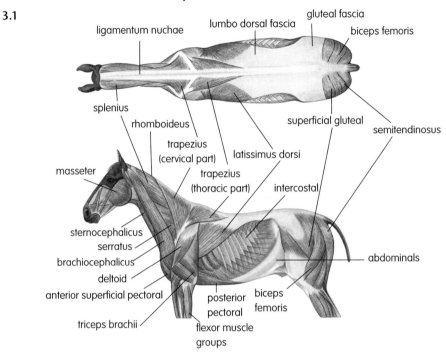

4. Know and understand the anatomical structure of the lower limbs

4. 1

Structure of the horse's leg below the knee

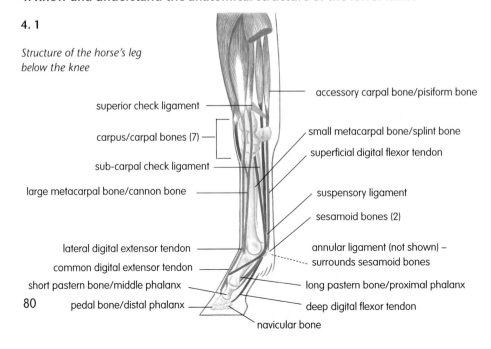

80

5. Understand lower limb abnormalities

5.1

Common lower limb abnormalities:

Splints are bony enlargement on splint/cannon bone. Caused by concussion, blows, hard work with young horses. The horse is not always lame, however pressure on splint will cause horse to flinch. Can be felt and seen. Once formed they usually do not cause problems as long as they do not interfere with joint action. Treatment is rest and cold water hosing, then light exercise on soft ground.

Navicular syndrome has no single known cause. Typified by degeneration of the navicular bone, possibly as a result of compression of the navicular bone under the deep digital flexor tendon, or tension on the ligaments that support the navicular bone. There is no single treatment, but correct foot balance, possible corrective shoeing (lifting the heels), less intense work, drugs to improve the blood flow may alleviate the effects.

Bone spavin is bony enlargement (osteoarthritis) on the lower, inner aspect of the hock. Caused by concussion, exertion or bad conformation (cow or sickle hocks). Spavin test will show lameness. Usually visible. Surgical shoeing, pain relief may alleviate the condition, but it is irreversible.

Ringbone is bony enlargement of the pastern. High ringbone affects the pastern joint; low ringbone, the coffin joint. Caused by concussion, strain, bad conformation, a direct blow. Sometimes horse is lame. Can sometimes be felt. X-ray confirms diagnosis. Condition is degenerative. Shoeing to support the heels may help. If near joint, horse may never be able to work; if not, horse may do light work when ringbone is formed.

Sidebone is ossification of the lateral cartilages. Caused by concussion, blow. Can be felt – cartilages become hard. Horse is not usually lame. Many horses get sidebone as they get older and there are few problems with them.

Sesamoiditis is inflammation of sesamoid bones in fetlock. Can affect the suspensory ligament. Caused by poor blood flow, excessive stress of fetlock, conformation. Evidenced by heat, swelling; diagnosis by X-ray. Rest. Vet will reestablish normal blood flow to the region using drugs.

Sprains and strains are injuries to ligament, tendon, muscle. Caused by slipping or pulling up suddenly, bad conformation, bad shoeing, heavy going, galloping a tired horse. Cause heat, swelling, pain, lameness. Basic treatment is rest, cold water hosing, ice packs, followed by controlled exercise. Modern treatments include the use of ultrasound, laser therapy and the use of stem cells.

The following names are specific types of such injuries:

A curb is a swelling below the point of hock around the tendons/ligaments. Caused by weak hocks, strain, injury to tendon/ligament. Can usually be seen. Consequences range from horse not being lame through to severe lameness. Treatment is mainly rest, followed by controlled exercise programme.

A bog spavin is a soft swelling of synovial fluid on the inside and to the front of the hock. Often does not cause lameness, but has an underlying cause, which could be excessive strain or conformation-related. Hose, try to find the cause.

A thoroughpin is a soft swelling just above the hock in the groove at the back of the leg, typified by inflammation of the deep digital flexor tendon. Caused by strain, poor conformation. May not cause lameness. Rest, hose.

A windgall is a soft swellings just above the fetlock, most commonly on hind legs, but can be all round. If only one leg is affected then there may be an issue in the joint. There are tendinous and articular types. Caused by strain, overwork conformation, breed type.. Usually do not cause lameness. Can hose.

6. Understand the principles for shoeing horses

6. 1

You should be prepared to discuss foot balance in the context of both the shod and unshod horse.

Lines demonstrating good balance and alignment of shoulder to pastern angle

Balanced foot and good hoof-pastern axis from side and front view

Broken back hoof-pastern axis; puts strain on the back of the leg

Broken forward hoof-pastern axis subjects lower limb and foot to more concussion

6.2

Look at the shoes and compare the wear of them. This should be even. If a shoe is worn more on one side than the other then there is a potential lameness problem in the future. If one front shoe is worn more than another then again there is a potential lameness issue. Look at the hind shoes – are the toes worn? This could mean the horse has joint issues, or it could be that he is lazy!

'Dumping' toes means that there is less bearing surface for the horse's weight on the ground and this should only be undertaken for remedial reasons.

6.3

Long toes and low heels can lead to strain on tendons and ligaments.

Look at the sole of the foot. There should be the same amount of foot either side of the frog and the shape of both sides should be similar.

6.4

Forefeet are rounded for weightbearing and hind feet are oval for pushing.

Many horses work unshod now as they only work on artificial surfaces.

Horses and ponies with strong hoof wall, may be able to work unshod on all terrain, but those with brittle wall or undertaking a lot of roadwork/rocky terrain will probably need to be shod for protection.

Pads can be utilised to help protect horses who are flatfooted or have thin soles. However, grit and small stones can work their way in under the pad and lead to corns/abscesses. Also shoes tend to become loose more quickly as the pad is between the foot and the shoe. Some pads can be filled with silicone to give greater protection and help keep grit out. Pads can help stop snow balling in the foot in winter. Be aware that some pads may be prone to causing slippage on some surfaces, such as worn metalled roads.

6.5

There are a variety of specialist shoes that can influence the balance and support of the foot. These may be fitted following consultation with vet and farrier to improve or alleviate a condition. Some examples are:

Bar shoe – looks like a hunter shoe with an added strip of metal across the heels. Supports heels and frog. Horse can be worked normally.

Egg-bar shoe – shoe looks a complete oval or 'egg' shape. The bar section extends beyond the heel, used remedially not for work, but often with box rest.

Raised heels – the end of the bars have an extension that lifts the heel, altering the balance of the foot. Used for navicular syndrome and laminitis; takes the pressure off the tendons.

Heart bar – wide weight-bearing shoe that looks like a 'heart' shape. Supports the pedal bone. Often used for laminitic conditions.

Broad web – wide weight-bearing surface, gives support to the wall and sole of the hoof. Can be slippery when horse is ridden.

Lateral and medial extensions – alter the weight-bearing surface and the loading of the limb when on the ground.

Plastic shoes – can be used for foals, horses with poor hoof growth. Usually glued on.

7. Know the structure and functions of the circulatory and respiratory systems

7. 1

The respiratory system:

Takes in oxygen, removes carbon dioxide (gaseous exchange).

Helps eliminate excess water, through evaporation of the water on the exhaled breath.
Helps with temperature control.
Allows the horse to communicate by making sound.
A horse can only breathe through his nose.

7.2
A horse's respiration rate increases for the following reasons:
When undertaking exercise.
As a result of fear, pain, stress.
As a result of fever/infection.

7.3
The circulatory system carries:
Oxygen from lungs to cells.
Carbon dioxide from cells to lungs.
Water and nutrients to cells.
Heat to the body surface.
Waste products to the kidneys.
Hormones from endocrine glands sending messages to various body parts.
Cells to contaminated sites to kill infection.

7.4
Problems associated with the circulatory system include anaemia, arrhythmia, heart disease, heart failure.

8. Know and understand the treatment of minor injuries and common aliments

8.1–8.2
For types and treatment of minor injuries, see **Stage 2, Unit 2a, 6.1–6.3.**
Common ailments include the following.

Colic: Pain in the digestive tract. Horses cannot be sick and they have a digestive tract that is susceptible to blockages.
Some causes – eating poor-quality food, eating unsuitable food, worm damage, stress, sudden change of diet, blockage.
Symptoms – can be mild (looking uncomfortable, off his food) through to thrashing around violently; sweating, looking at his sides, getting up and down are also often seen.
Treatment – call the vet. If possible put horse in a large box with big banks. Remove

food and water. Vet may administer a muscle relaxant and any other medication necessary to support the pain management and healing process.

Azoturia: Also known as tying up, equine rhabdomyolysis syndrome (ER), and recurrent equine rhabdomyolysis syndrome (RER).
Causes – result of poorly managed feeding and exercise related to the individual horse, or possible genetic predisposition (RER). Once developed this condition is often recurs and needs consistent monitoring. Too much glycogen in the muscles creates more lactic acid than can be taken away by the blood. Horses with selenium and vitamin E deficiency are prone. Certain breeds appear to be prone.
Symptoms – shortly after exercise has started, the horse becomes reluctant to go forward, the muscles in the hindquarters go stiff. Pain and sweating.
Treatment – cease work immediately. Keep the hindquarters warm. Get transport if not at home. Call the vet. Rest and laxative diet. Feed regime regulated. Exercise daily.

Laminitis: Inflammation of the sensitive laminae of the foot.
Causes – too much rich grass, concussion, stress, carbohydrate overloading, retention of placenta after foaling.
Symptoms – standing with weight on hind legs and forefeet stretched out. Reluctance to walk. Increased digital pulse in foot. Condition generally affects forefeet. Pedal bone may sink and rotate.
Treatment – the vet will probably give painkillers. Encourage horse to walk with gentle in-hand exercise. Farrier may undertake corrective shoeing. Feed regime strictly monitored. Once contracted a horse/pony will be susceptible to recurrence.

Mud fever: Can affect all of lower leg both front and back.
Causes – bacteria invading skin that has become softened.
Symptoms – swelling, heat, pain. Skin has scabs. Hair can fall off. Horse can be lame.
Treatment – wash with antibacterial shampoo. Dry thoroughly. Clip hair away. Use antibiotic ointment. Dispose of scabs carefully. Once contracted, horse will be susceptible.

Sweet itch: Allergic condition.
Cause – hypersensitive reaction to allergens in the saliva of midges.
Symptoms – rubbing and scratching mane and tail area leading to broken hair, broken/bleeding skin, bald patches, trauma.
Treatment – prevention is better. Keep animal away from areas where midges are likely to congregate. Use insecticides (benzyl benzoate is the best known). Fit special anti-midge rugs which cover the areas likely to be affected.

Ringworm: Highly contagious condition that can be caught by humans.

Cause – fungal infection.

Symptoms – raised tufts of hair, not always circular in appearance. Horse may be itchy and will scratch.

Treatment – isolate, call the vet. Apply antifungal shampoo (suitable PPE should be used). Destroy bedding and disinfect all equipment and the stables, which in addition can be fumigated as the fungal spores can remain dormant for a long time.

Strangles: Highly contagious condition.

Cause – bacterial disease.

Symptoms – temperature rise, horse dull, discharge from nose, coughing, glands under jaw become swollen, hot and painful and abscesses form.

Treatment – isolate. Call the vet – antibiotics will be given. Sick nurse and isolation procedures; keep nostrils clean.

8.3

A well-stocked first aid cabinet will include: round-ended scissors, bowl, cotton wool, towel, antibacterial scrub, ready-to-use poultice, Gamgee, a variety of bandages, antibiotic spray, Vaseline, wound powder, thermometer, vet's phone number.

8.4

Isolation procedure:

Remove the horse to isolation box, which should be well ventilated and have a good deep bed with banks.

If possible he should be able to see other horses.

Bedding from the original box should be burnt and the box disinfected.

Equipment used regularly with the horse should be disinfected. Keep equipment that is being used for sick horse separate from other feed bowls, grooming kit and tack.

Place disinfectant bath outside box.

If possible, one person to look after the horse.

Overalls and gloves for groom.

Vet's instructions should be carried out to the letter including administering medicines.

Constant supply of fresh water.

Feeding as advised by the vet. Succulents and small feeds to tempt horse to eat.

Do not over-groom or fuss the horse.

Keep a written record of TPR and general improvement.

Unit 3a: The principles of feeding and fittening horses

1. Understand the composition of food and its value in the horse's diet

1.1

Food is the source of energy and other essential nutrients. It is needed for the maintenance of life, growth and/or work and for the repair of tissue.
Nutrients in the horse's diet:

- Protein – for body building.
- Carbohydrates – for energy (starches, sugars and fibre).
- Fats and oils – horses can digest vegetable oils efficiently.
- Vitamins A,D,E,K (fat-soluble), B complex and C (water-soluble).
- Minerals – calcium, phosphorous, potassium, sodium, sulphur, chlorine, magnesium (macro minerals); zinc, manganese, iron, fluorine, iodine, selenium, cobalt, copper, (micro-minerals).
- Water – between 65 and 70 per cent of the horse's body is water.

1.2

A balanced diet provides all the nutrients a horse requires for his lifestyle in appropriate amounts relevant to each other. This helps keep him in optimum health.
A horse needs approximately 2 ½ per cent his bodyweight in feed daily.
A 16hh horse weighs approximately 500kg (1100lb).
2½ per cent is approximately 13 kg (28lb) feed per day.
A horse in medium work would be on approximately 25 per cent hard feed = 3.25 kg (7lb) feed per day. This could be split into two feeds per day. The rest in bulk (hay, haylage and/or grass).
Type of hard feed depends on temperament, work done, breed, ability of rider, and quality of bulk.

1.3

Water is essential for life and health. It is needed for: digestion, blood and lymph, urine and faeces, fluid in the eyes, temperature regulation, respiration, synovial fluid, milk (for lactating mares). It is lost through natural functions e.g. urination, digestion, sweating, stress.
Horses need between 8½ and 10 gallons (38–45 litres) per day.

1.4

The value of the main elements of feed are as follows.

Grass is the horse's natural food. Good-quality grass contains all the nutriments for a horse. It is often called Dr Green as it can improve a horse's condition after winter, or an illness.

Concentrates, depending on their nutritional value, offer a horse more carbohydrate and protein if they are working hard or are breeding stock. Grass alone may not provide such horses with enough energy to perform successfully.

Bulk/roughage is essential to ensure that the digestive system continues to work efficiently. In the wild the digestive system is kept full because horses would graze some 18 hours per day. This needs to be replicated with domesticated horses.

1.5

Some issues that may affect a horse's diet include quality of food, routine, work to be undertaken, time of year, temperament, age, breed and type. The general health and welfare of the individual horse should also be considered, especially in cases of metabolic disorders.

2. Understand how to organise a feed room

2.1

Effective organisation of a feed room includes:
Convenient location.
Access to water, electricity.
A clear feed chart.
Shelf for additives/equipment.
Food being used in rotation.
Vermin-proof bins.
Swept daily.
Utensils (bowls, spoons, scoops) cleaned daily.
A dry environment is ideal; damp or humid conditions will compromise the effective shelf-life of feed, and possibly its quality.

2.2

Management of feedstuffs:
One person should be responsible for ordering new feed, and records should be kept.
Order stock so that it can be used before the 'use by' date.
Use by rotation. Do not keep putting new food on top of old in feed bins.
Vermin-proof storage.

3. Understand how to get horses fit

3.1

To get a horse fit for medium work takes approximately 12 weeks. The first 8 weeks are the same as for the fittening programme for Stage 2 (see **Stage 2, Unit 3a, 6.1–6.3**).

Weeks eight to twelve:
The horse needs to go to small competitions for experience and to help his mental state. Factor into the programme the weather and time of year.
Hacking and schooling need to continue. Canters and hand gallops may need to be longer depending on where his fitness is and where it needs to be. Testing the horse's fitness with a pipe-opener will let you know if longer and faster canters are necessary. Feed should be adjusted accordingly. The horse may well be on 60 per cent bulk 40 per cent hard feed.

3.2

The value of different gaits and exercises is as follows.
Walk – tones muscles, hardens ligaments and tendons without stress. Helps build up stamina.
Trot – increases demands made the on horse. Further strengthens tendons, ligaments and muscles.
Canter – increases cardio-vascular efficiency. Muscles, tendons and ligaments are toned.
Riding uphill – makes the heart and lungs work harder. Encourages the horse to use his hindquarters more.
Riding downhill – helps with balance.
Short gallops – 'pip- openers' – assess level of fitness. Length of time taken to recover shows level of fitness.
Lungeing – is a useful alternative once a basic level of fittening is established. Useful to see how horse is progressing. It is harder work for the horse than most ridden work so can be a fitness indicator.
Schooling in the exercises that are appropriate to the horse's level of training will help develop strength, suppleness and obedience.

3.3

Fittening programmes may vary according to the demands of different types of competition.
For show classes horses need to have a good covering of flesh, but not be overweight. The show horse does not need to be as fit as an eventer. However, a show hunter must be able to gallop without undue strain on his heart, legs and lungs.

Eventers need to have canter/gallop work included within their training regime; this may be through interval training or traditional training depending upon available facilities.

For endurance riding, after the usual initial training the horse needs distance and speed to be slowly increased before introducing faster work. Hill work is very useful. Slow, steady work will increase endurance and stamina.

Schooling will improve balance and co-ordination and is beneficial for show horses, hunters, etc., not just dressage horses, showjumpers and eventers.

Relate work to the individual horse's conformation to minimise risk of injury.

3.4

Factor in rest and recovery sessions within any training programme.

Hacking to maintain basic fitness and support relaxation between schooling sessions.

Evaluate competition results and adjust schooling programme to incorporate additional skill training to improve future performance.

Continue to monitor recovery rates within fitness regimes. Fast work should be carried out every three days to suit the individual (progression/maintenance/performance).

3.5

Fitness indicators in the horse include:

Enthusiasm and energy levels for work.

Respiratory and heart rate recovery rates should return to normal quickly.

Horse should not be stiff after exercise.

Horse should not sweat excessively whilst working.

You should factor in the temperament of the individual horse, as some can be more enthusiastic than others, regardless of their fitness levels – 'keen' is not necessarily the same thing as 'fit'.

3.6

Issues that may affect a fittening programme include:

Weather and environmental factors such as wind, fog, snow and ice.

Ground conditions – too hard, too soft, dusty.

Horse injury or illness – minor or serious.

Rider injury, illness, work commitments.

Unit 3b: The principles of stabling and grassland care for horses

1. Know about different types of stable design and construction

1.1
Refer to **Stage 2, Unit 3b, 1.1–1.2.**

1.2
The requirement to compare different types of drainage and ventilation will include the ability to discuss and compare these facilities after a visual assessment of them has been made. See **Stage 2, Unit 3b, 1.3–1.4** for further details.

1.3
There should be as few fixtures and fittings as practical: a tie ring at breast height, a haynet ring, possibly mineral lick holder, but must be kept full.

Some stables have mangers that can have the hard food put in and then turned round into the box. The horse is eating at an abnormal height, but it does save having to go into the box with hard feed.

Automatic waterers are labour-saving, but must be cleaned daily, may freeze in winter unless supply pipe is insulated/trace-heated. Can't monitor how much the horse is drinking unless metering fitted. Supply pipe should be concealed or at least protected. Water buckets are labour-intensive and can be kicked over. Sometimes kept in a tyre, but this takes up a lot of room. Can see how much is being drunk.

There should be protective bars on the window, a kick bolt as well as a bolt on the door, light switch outside the box where the horse cannot reach it.

Light source should be out of horse's reach, and protected.

1.4
Placement of certain horses on a yard may be dependent on factors such as:

Suitability of the stable – location, size.

Bedding type – supports respiratory considerations if dust free.

Relationship with neighbouring horses.

Aspect – quiet or busy placement within the yard, near feed room, reception area.

Stallions, mares and young stock may not suit being next to each other and need separation.

Consider the location of isolation boxes within the yard complex.

2. Understand horse welfare and behaviour when stabled

2.1
To gain a stabled horse's confidence:
Try to maintain a regular routine.
Be consistent in your reactions.
Be positive but not aggressive in your behaviour.
Take time to get to know the horse and his normal behaviour.

2.2
Stereotypical behaviour – is the activity other than the horse's normal behaviour repertoire. Main forms are:
Crib-biting (grabbing hold of something and taking in air).
Wind-sucking (taking in air without grabbing hold of anything).
Box-walking.
Weaving.
Shaking the head.

These used to be called 'vices' and it used to be thought that horses learn these behaviours by copying others. Modern research shows that other factors such as too much hard feed and not enough bulk, over-training, lack of social interaction and not being turned out enough with others all play a part. The yard environment may also be a stressor for an individual horse. Horses who display stereotypical behaviour may have ulcers, may be difficult to keep condition on, and may suffer from issues related to the behaviour – e.g. crib-biters may wear their teeth down and not be able to tear off grass/hay adequately.

2.3
To control stereotypical behaviour, ensure horses are turned out for long periods daily, if possible with others, that they have free access to bulk food and are not overfed hard food. Some people use an anti-cribbing collar for crib-biters and wind-suckers. Surfaces can be covered with foul tasting (approved) liquid/products on areas likely to be grabbed. An anti-weaving grille can be used on the stable door for a weaver.

3. Know and understand health and safety procedures and relevant legislation

3.1–3.2
Yards should have a health and safety policy to guide persons to behave appropriately and reduce their risk of injury

There should be risk assessments for all tasks – these minimise the risk of injury to self and others, and highlight the need for correct training and practice.

Yards should have a specific fire safety risk assessment and a fire safety procedure.

There should be an accident procedure capable of being implemented when an accident has occurred and needs attention.

Safety warning and advisory signs highlight areas of potential hazard, danger or need for vigilance.

3.3

Fire procedure is explained in **Stage 1, Unit 3, 1.3**.

3.4

A risk assessment should identify the hazards present (or any that may have the potential to develop) when undertaking a task, and the extent of the risks. A hazard has the potential to cause harm. A risk is the likelihood that the harm from the hazard will be realised.

All this is to try to ensure the safety of clients, staff and equines. Non-compliance can mean prosecution if negligence can be proved.

4. Understand the management of grassland and pasture for horses

4.1

Good grazing – not overgrazed, good grasses, droppings picked up, rested on rotation. Be able to identify and name good grasses.

4.2

An annual plan for pasture management:

Winter: Many people rest the pasture, as damaged ground may not produce good grass in the spring/summer. Some people use 'sacrifice' paddocks that the horses can wreck and which can recover in the spring. Poorly drained paddocks should not be grazed in winter. Horses/ponies who live out all winter tend not to damage the ground so much.

Spring: When dry enough the ground can be harrowed and rolled. Poached areas can be re-seeded. It is not advisable to plough and re-seed a field as the field will be out of action for up to a year. Soil analysis can be taken and fertiliser applied as required. Horses must not graze until the fertiliser is washed in. Repair fences as necessary. Weeds can be sprayed in spring (but then do not graze for several weeks). Watch out for laminitis if grass grows quickly and/or strongly. Can divide field and rotate grazing every three weeks.

Summer: Continue rotation grazing. Pick up droppings daily. If not possible then harrow the fields frequently when the weather and ground conditions are appropriate (ideally dry and sunny) . Pull and burn ragwort. Field may need topping.

Autumn: Can get a flush of grass in early autumn, so watch ponies for signs of obesity or laminitis. Fertiliser like Farm Yard Manure (FYM) can be applied, as it will break down during winter. Acorns need to be picked up if possible. Drainage ditches need to be cleared ready for winter.

4.3
Cross-grazing with sheep or cattle is useful – they will eat the grass horses will not. This will also assist in reducing the equine worm burden as the worms do not affect sheep in the same way as horses.
Fencing must be taken into consideration if cross-grazing is undertaken. The fencing must suit the individual animals and may need to be taken up or down before re-grazing: this may apply to sheep netting or electric cattle fencing.
Cattle will poach the ground more than sheep.

5. Understand horse welfare and behaviour when at grass
When turned out, horses are living as near as possible to how they would in the wild, especially if they are with others. They will graze and wander around, play and socialise. This will help to keep them happy and content. It will also help to keep the digestive system working.

5.1–5.2
Dominant horse may be aggressive to other horse or humans when turned out. There may be In-fighting with others if in a group – kicks and bites.
Timid horses may get bullied.
Older horse may be slow to react to younger more energetic ones.
Mares and gelding together may result in fighting, kicks and bites. Mares may become more aggressive when in season.
Avoid mixing foals and yearlings with more mature horses.
Horses in summer may be unsettled by flies and heat.
Horses in winter may become cold and unsettled, or lethargic.
It is not natural behaviour for a horse in company to be standing on his own or lying down a long time – this needs cheeking.

Unit 4: Lunge a fit horse for exercise

1. Be able to promote and maintain a safe working environment

1.1

Assess the situation – ground, effect of the weather, arena security (gates and fencing), other people and horses being lunged.

2. Be able to lunge a fit horse for exercise

2.1–2.3

As for riding you must practise, practise, practise.

Make sure you can use the equipment efficiently and effectively.

Ensure you stand in the correct position.

Warm up on both reins without side-reins in all three gaits, unless the horse is being naughty (in which case put side-reins on early).

Once the horse is going forward, attach the side-reins and ensure they are of a length that will encourage the horse to go forward into them, but does not restrict their movement.

Use transitions and make the circle smaller and larger to encourage the horse to improve his way of going.

Take note of the horse's rhythm and balance, as you will probably be asked to discuss these in the overall evaluation of the session. Be able to discuss the use and fit of the equipment, the horse's response to you, his stiffer side, the size and shape of circle used and why you did what you did.

Build up a relationship with the horse and be quick to recognise his temperament and lunge accordingly. You must be experienced and confident enough to be able to adjust your lungeing technique to the horse.

3. Understand why and how horses are lunged

3.1

The evaluation needs to consider:

Did the horse go forwards?

Did the horse maintain a rhythm – walk, trot, canter and on both reins?

Which rein was his more supple?

What was the contact (and straightness) on both reins?
Was the horse obedient to your aids and your exercises used?
Has the horse worked?

3.2
Benefits of lungeing and long reining. (Be prepared to discuss the benefits of long reining although you will not be expected to demonstrate.)

Benefits of lungeing:
Can be used as part of backing.
It can improve the way of going and provide visual evidence of how the horse's way of going is improving.
If time is short, lungeing can fulfil daily exercise in less time than riding.
Useful exercise when no rider is available.
Useful as a change for exercise.
Can settle a fresh horse.
Good for discipline.
Can introduce a horse to poles and a jump.
Useful exercise for a horse with a saddle sore/girth gall.

Benefits of long reining:
Helps young horses to understand aids from behind.
Allows young horses to be worked outside a school before being ridden.
Start for driving and racehorses and, indeed, any young horse.
Horse learns to go forward without a lead.
May enhance horse's way of going.
Can be used to teach advanced dressage movements.

3.3
A horse who works on the lunge without rhythm and balance is likely to do damage to his limbs and injure himself.
The tempo of the rhythm must suit the horse, his education and the size of circle that it is worked on.

3.4
Lungeing equipment that is a poor fit is uncomfortable and potentially dangerous to the horse's safety and well-being.
It can cause rubs and sores. For example, a loose cavesson can rub the outside eye, cause injury or discomfort and a change in behaviour.

Tack that is too tight may induce tension and possible panic (e.g. side-reins too short). Incorrectly fitted boots may slip, fall down or trip the horse.

3.5

The benefits of correct lungeing equipment:

The cavesson will provide a direct contact for the lunge line to be attached without negatively influencing the contact on the horse's mouth. Ideally the noseband on the bridle will have been removed to support this.

A good lunge line will be of a suitable length to allow the lunger to be able to lunge the horse on a suitable circle.

The lunge whip should be easy to hold and have a lash that can be controlled by the lunger; neither too heavy nor too short.

Boots protect the horse's legs when working on circles of various sizes; particularly relevant if the horse is shod.

Overreach boots can be used in addition to protect the horse from striking into his forefeet when working on the circle.

Side-reins enable the horse to work into a contact, which will support his balance and enable him to work more effectively.

PTT Revision Notes

Class Lesson: Coach a group of riders for improvement

The best way to prepare yourself is to watch good teachers and practise, practise, practise.

This may be a flatwork or a jumping session. You will be told which one you are teaching at the morning briefing. All lesson plans should be prepared in order to teach any selected session.

1. Be able to coach safely and efficiently

1.1 –1.2
At all times consider the safety of:
The riders.
The horses.
Yourself.
Be prepared to use your time efficiently.

2. Be able to produce a lesson plan

2.1
Bring lesson plans for all the lesson briefs to the exam. Pay particular attention to the open lesson plans (flat and jump). This is a plan for a lesson the candidate feels would be suitable for riders they have not assessed before. The plan may list a selection of exercises that could be used up to Stage 2 level riders. The candidate should then select those exercises that are relevant to the riders and, as with any lesson plan, this may need adjusting on the exam day, depending on the type of riders, horses and how they progress.

To produce a lesson plan, split it into three sections: introduction/assessment; main content; cool down/summary. List the resources you require and the aims of the lesson. There should be space at the bottom for feedback from the riders and self-evaluation.

The lesson plan will, of necessity, be generic, but it will give you a basic structure and a foundation to work from with some suitable exercises.

3. Be able to prepare the coaching environment

3.1–3.3

Check the arena for suitability and safety. You may not be the first person to use the arena.

Check the surface and comment to the assessor if you have any concerns.

Check gate/entrance is shut.

Discuss with the assessor any concerns over the safety of the lesson, weather (wind, rain, heat).

Tidy materials (jumps, poles) or set them out for your lesson plan. Take cups off wings.

Check the tack and equipment of the horse and the rider before commencing the lesson.

4. Be able to assess a group of riders

4.1

Introduce yourself and find out your rider's names and abilities. Ask if they know the horse they are riding. Tell the ride your brief (this may include the general theme of the lesson and your intended format/structure) and then ask them if there is anything they would particularly like to work on. Be confident but not bossy.

4.2 and 4.4

Warm up the ride and assess them. Open or closed order depending on what they are used to.

The assessor will then probably discuss with you how you feel the session will progress. This is the time when you can discuss the suitability of your plan.

4.3

Make simple evaluations on the safety and standard of the riders.

Are they safe on this horse on this day?

Who is the strongest rider and why?

Who is the weakest rider and why?

Which horse/rider combination is going as lead file?

Will you be working the ride in open or closed order as a result of your evaluations?

5. Be able to coach a group of riders for improvement

5.1–5.5

Commence your lesson as planned. Assess the general competence and safety of the riders and horses. Discuss this with the assessor after you have worked them in.

Give your full attention to the riders.

Consider where you should stand in order to be clearly heard by the riders and the assessor.

Use suitable exercises to develop your lesson plan. If the plan has altered then adapt your exercises to meet the session aims.

Throughout the session offer opinion (technical discussion) and invite feedback on the riders' positions and their ability to ride the horses and maintain a safe, correct position.

Encourage the riders to provide feedback to you by asking them open questions.

The lesson must be safe, interactive but must also help the riders work towards improving their riding skills. It should be fun where possible.

Allow the horses and riders an opportunity to warm down.

Hint for flatwork lessons:
Use creative but safe movements

Hints for jumping lessons:
Warm up the ride with stirrup leathers at jumping length.

Maximum jump height 76cm (2ft 6in).

If teaching a jumping lesson make sure your distances are correct for the horses you have. You must know all your jump distances and be confident walking them.

Try to keep the ride moving or, if standing still, get them to observe each other jumping and discuss this.

Only allow riders to jump if you are watching them.

Avoid saying 'good' after each jump – give structured feedback, what was good or what they need to do next time to be better.

6. Be able to evaluate the coaching session

6.1

For your conclusion provide feedback to the group as a whole and individually.

6.2

State the future progression of this session with this group of riders. This will formulate an action plan. This will then be the basis of the next session's lesson plan.

6.3

The assessor will then discuss the lesson with you. Be honest with your self-reflection. This should include:

The rider's ability and improvements.

Your own delivery of the session. Would you do anything differently if you taught the session again?

6.4

From your reflection of the delivered session consider how you can improve your own skills to advance your personal coaching practice.

Individual lesson: Coach an inexperienced rider for improvement

This may be a lunge or a lead rein session. Prepare a generic lesson plan for each session.

1. Be able to coach safely and efficiently

1.1
At all times consider the safety of:
The riders.
The horses.
Yourself.

2. Be able to produce a session plan

2.1
Bring lesson plans for all the lesson briefs to the exam: prepare an open lesson plan for both the lunge and the lead rein lesson.
This is a plan for a lesson the candidate feels would be suitable for riders they have not assessed before. The plan may list a selection of exercises that could be used for up to Stage 2 level riders. The candidate should then select those exercises that are relevant to the rider and, as with any lesson plan, this may need adjusting on the exam day, depending on the type of rider, horse and how they progress.
To produce a lesson plan, split it into three sections: introduction/assessment; main content; cool down/summary. List the resources you require and the aims of the lesson. There should be space at the bottom for feedback from the rider and self-evaluation.
The lesson plan will, of necessity, be generic, but it will give you a basic structure and a foundation to work from with some suitable exercises.

3. Be able to prepare the coaching environment

3.1–3.3
Check the arena for suitability and safety. You may not be the first person to use the arena.
Check surface and comment to the assessor if you have any concerns.
Check gate/entrance is shut.

Discuss with the assessor any concerns over the safety of the lesson, weather (wind, rain, heat).

Check the tack and equipment of the horse, rider and any materials used before commencing the lesson.

4. Be able to assess an inexperienced rider

4.1

Introduce yourself and find out your rider's name and ability. This may be a child for the lead rein lesson so consider your body language, voice tone and words used. Ask if they know the horse/pony they are riding and briefly check the tack and stirrup length. Introduce your rider to the aims of the lesson and then ask them if there is anything they would particularly like to work on. Be confident but not bossy.

4.2 and 4.4

The assessor will then probably discuss with you how you feel the session will progress. This is the time when you can discuss the suitability of your plan in context to the specific horse and rider.

4.3

Make simple evaluations on the safety and standard of the rider.

Do they look and appear safe and confident on the horse/pony?

What are their positional strengths and why?

What are their positional weaknesses and why?

5. Be able to coach an inexperienced rider for improvement

5.1–5.5

Commence your lesson as planned. Assess the general competence and safety of the rider and horse. Discuss this with the assessor after you have assessed them.

Give your full attention to the rider.

Use suitable exercises to develop your lesson plan. If the plan has altered then adapt your exercises to meet the session aims.

Throughout the session offer opinion (technical discussion) and invite feedback on the rider's positions and their ability to ride the horse/pony and maintain a safe correct position. Encourage the rider to provide feedback to you by asking them open questions.

The lesson must be safe, interactive but must also help the rider work towards improving their riding skills. It should be fun where possible.

Lunge session:

Introduce yourself and ask the rider to stand in a safe position while you warm up the horse. Find out their riding experience. They may be a beginner.

Do not ignore the rider while warming up the horse – make conversation with them.

The horse should be warmed-up, so lunge briefly on one rein without the side-reins and then on the other rein with the side-reins. Check the tack. Make sure there is a neck strap. This must be done very quickly and efficiently.

Mount the rider. Check their stirrups are equal and the leathers are of suitable length. Assess their position and use suitable exercises to help them improve. Do not get the rider to undertake exercises that are not suitable for their issues. Give praise where it is due. Be enthusiastic but not overbearing.

The session must be interesting and the rider must be kept involved with the use of open questions. A rapport with the rider must be built up.

At the end of the session provide feedback and a future plan for the rider.

You will then be asked to evaluate and self-reflect on the session with the assessor.

Lead rein session:

The rider may be an adult beginner or a young person who has ridden a little.

Find out how much they have done. Build up a rapport with them.

It is important to practise leading a rider and teaching them at the same time. This is a real skill.

Mount and assess them. Make sure they mount and dismount correctly.

Check their stirrups are level.

If they are a complete beginner it may be useful to tie a knot in the reins and get them to hold the neck strap or pommel.

Undertake exercises that will help them to improve and keep them interested.

Be enthusiastic, but remember you are close to the rider and if you are too loud it will put them off.

When trotting ask for sitting trot first.

The session must be interesting and the rider must be kept involved with the use of open questions and praise where it is due.

If they are assessed as being competent they may be taken off the lead rein. Walk closely with them initially and then encourage them to ride by themselves.

At the end of the session provide feedback and a future plan for the rider.

You will be asked to evaluate and self-reflect on the session with the assessor. Be realistic and relevant.

With both sessions safety is important but must not be used as an excuse for a poor session.

6. Be able to evaluate the coaching session

6.1

For your conclusion, provide feedback to the rider.

6.2

State the future progression of this session with this rider. This will formulate an action plan. This will then be the basis of the next session's lesson plan.

6.3

The assessor will then discuss the lesson with you. Be honest with your self-reflection. This should include:

The rider's ability and improvements.

Your own delivery of the session. Would you do anything differently if you taught the session again?

6.4

From your reflection of the delivered session consider how you can improve your own skills to advance your personal coaching practice.

Theory Unit (TU) 1: Understanding the fundamentals of coaching sport

This unit is assessed at the same time at unit 2. This is usually in a classroom situation. They are assessed using discussion and through your knowledge of equestrian terms and suitable terminology.

Theory unit 1 assesses your understanding of the importance of planning, implementing, analysing and revising coaching sessions. You should also be able to develop learning, performance and manage the rider(s)' behaviour within the lessons.

1. Understand the role of a coach

1.1–1.13

You should be able to discuss:

How to put the riders at the centre of the process – they are having the session, not you.

Structuring the sessions around the individual's needs – check that you know their needs, short- and long-term.

Motivate and empower the riders – what do they want and how are you going to help them achieve it?

Explain any rules and regulations that support good and best practice – e.g. school rules, etiquette.

When developing a positive and professional coach: rider relationship, put respect first – friendship may come later. Consider child: adult differences.

2. Understand the coaching process

2.1– 2.18

You should be able to discuss:

Handling of confidential information – data protection.

How to meet the individual rider's needs – support them to achieve.

How to plan work for both horse and rider, how to structure a session – timings, challenges and rest periods.

SMART goal setting.

Developing of listening skills, when to demonstrate – confirming understanding

When a session may need to be adapted and why.

How to organise group sessions – consider all individual needs, the noisy one and the quiet rider.

3. Understand participant(s)' learning styles

3.1–3.6

You should be able to discuss:

Different learning styles and how to ensure they are all catered for – activist, reflector etc.

Differences in how adults and children learn – use of your language?

How to encourage riders to take responsibility for their own learning.

Management of different styles within private and group lessons.

How to monitor and evaluate learning – methods: verbal, written feedback, video use.

4. Understand behaviour management

4.1–4.10

You should be able to discuss:

A code of practice for riding in groups and one to one – school rules and regulations.

Maintaining positive relationships – keep professional, be polite.

How to encourage and reward positive behaviour – use of praise.

How to develop self-esteem within your riders.

How to respond to discriminatory behaviour and procedures to be followed.

5. Understand how to reflect on a coaching session

5. 1–5.7

You should be able to:

Provide self-reflection and future development needs – what did you do and how did you do it?

Discuss where and how feedback can be obtained – mentor, colleague, clients.

Discuss methods for personal action planning – set timescales for future planning.

Measure your own performance within your ability as a coach.

Discuss how to meet the rider's development needs.

Discuss how to ensure quality of delivery within the lessons – feedback and reflection for self.

Theory Unit (TU) 2: Understanding how to develop participant(s) through coaching sport

This assesses your understanding of the principles of planning, delivering and evaluating coaching sessions to improve riders' performance.

1. Understand the principles of planning coaching sessions

1.1–1.10

You should be able to discuss:

Information required from new riders and what is confidential – personal data, rider registration details.

Health and safety issues in various situations – you are responsible for the safety of the rider/horse and yourself. How are you able to react when a situation changes?

How to establish goals and progression for the rider – are they your goals or theirs; is the timing and achievement realistic, SMART.

Different coaching styles and when you might use them – alternating your style within a session to met the needs of all riders and keep the session fresh and alive.

How to make sessions fun and why this is important – engagement of the rider(s).

Why sessions might be adapted and how – things may change, adaptability, progressions or consolidation.

You may need to include the use of assistants to support the delivery of your sessions.

2. Understand the principles of skill development through coaching sessions

2.1–2.8

You should be able to discuss:

What are skill coordination, motor skill learning, skill acquisition, skill retention and transfer? How does this change if working with children, adults?

What might affect the development of a rider's skills? Consider learning types, fitness, fatigue, age, etc.

How to develop a rider's skills – physical (posture and position, fitness) and psychological (confidence levels).

The importance of gaining feedback from riders – how do you know they understand what you are asking; are they learning anything?

3. Understand how the stages of participant(s)' development impacts on their coaching

3.1–3.4
You should be able to discuss:

Progressive stages of an individual's development and how this affects what is coached and the coaching environment. This may be different for children and adults. Delivery may alter in a private or group lesson.

The influence and differences between training and competing.

4. Understand the principles of evaluation in coaching

4.1–4.7
You should be able to discuss:

How to cater for each individual – understand their needs and what information they need.

How to offer constructive feedback – what to say and when to say it.

Why evaluation is important – how did the lesson go? What would you do differently or the same?

Different evaluation methods – verbal, written feedback, video use.

Other people who can contribute to evaluation and potential issues – use of mentor?

Personal action planning – where are you going now?

Theory Unit (TU) 3: Supporting participants' lifestyle through coaching sport

This unit is assessed through pre-prepared presentations. All presentation should be prepared prior to the day and one will be selected for you to deliver. The other (pre-prepared plans) will be looked at by the assessor.

Each presentation should last up to 10 minutes and must be interactive.

For each presentation there are suggested topics you could choose.

1. Understand basic nutrition and hydration principles for sports performance

1. 1–1.6

This is assessed through the pre-prepared topic of:

Nutritional advice for novice riders.

The healthy plate.

The five different food types.

Hydration – the signs and symptoms of dehydration.

How best to achieve optimum nutrition and hydration before, during and after a session.

The principles of weight management for horse riders.

2. Understand physical conditioning for sport

2.1–2.8

This is assessed through the pre-prepared topic of the importance of warming up and cooling down for riders and horses:

- Reasons for warming up and cooling down.
- Injury prevention.
- Enhancing recovery time.
- Suitable exercises on the ground.
- Suitable mounted exercises.
- How warming up and cooling down can speed recovery time.
- Safety considerations when warming up fresh horses.
- Safety considerations when warming up novice riders.
- How to recognise when horse and rider are warmed up enough.
- The use of stretching exercises.
- Relating warm up to the work to be undertaken.

The physical requirements and conditioning for horse riding:
- The components of physical fitness.
- The components of skill related fitness.
- Physical requirements for riding.
- Methods of training the different physical components of riding.
- Basic anatomy and biomechanical demands of different riding activities.
- Testing available to assess fitness.

3. Understand principles of mental preparation in sport

3.1–3.5

This is assessed through the pre-prepared topic of mental preparation for riding – the mental capabilities required for a riding related activity.

Key methods for improving riders – confidence, concentration, emotional control, commitment.

The principles of rider development in the different stages of cognitive, emotional and social development:
- How a coach can profile a rider's mental skills.
- Basic coach intervention techniques for developing mental skills for training and competition.

4. Understand how to support participation awareness of drugs in sport

4.1–4.3

This is assessed through the pre-prepared topic of drug awareness in riding:
- The ethical issues surrounding taking drugs in sport.
- Setting an example for a rider.
- Where to find information about drugs in sport.
- What a competitor must do if taking supplements or prescription medicine.

Theory Unit (TU) 4: Understanding the principles of safe and equitable coaching practice

This unit assesses the coach's understanding of how to ensure that their coaching practice is safe and equitable.

1. Understanding how to ensure participant(s)' safety during sport-specific coaching sessions

1.1 – 1.11
To include topics such as:
Health and safety requirements, the rules of the school.
How to minimise risk of injury.
Possible external influences and how to deal with them
How to protect children from abuse.
Insurance requirements of a coach.

2. Understand how to ensure equitable coaching of sport-specific activities

2.1 – 2.12
To include topics such as:
Requirements impacting on equitable coaching.
Codes of practice for coaching riding.
Safe opportunities for disabled riders.
The using of support staff/helpers.

For both learning outcomes use the websites to be up to date with the latest information:
Sports Coach UK: www.sportscoachuk.org
Drug Use: www.feicleansport.org
FEI: www.fei.org
BrianMac Sports Coach: www.brianmac.co.uk
Business balls: www.businessballs.com